POLLUTED!

MY SOBER JOURNEY

POLLUTED!
MY SOBER JOURNEY

ALCOHOL, ADDICTION
AND THE 7 STAGES TO
GETTING CLEAN

DIRK FOSTER

Connect With Me:

Join My Newsletter and Receive a FREE BOOK at **www.thesoberjourney.com**

Facebook:
www.facebook.com/sobertravels/

Author Page:
https://www.facebook.com/Dirk-Foster-Author105017227522728/?modal=admin_todo_tour

Other Books by Dirk Foster:

The Sober Journey: A Guide to Prayer and Meditation in Recovery

Sober Body: A Guide to Health and Fitness in Sobriety

Sober and Broke: How to Make Money, Save Money, Pay Debt and Find Financial Peace is Sobriety

DEDICATION

For Paul Carafotes the man who brought me back to life.

I can never thank you enough.

And to all the people in the world still struggling to get clean.

Never give up.

WHY YOU MIGHT NEED THIS BOOK

Do you feel that you drink too much or too often? Is drinking (or drug use) causing drama or negativity in your life? Are there negative consequences from your drinking? Are you tired of hangovers? Does your life sometimes feel out of control because of drinking? Do you wish you could stop drinking or slow down? Do you worry that you won't have any fun without drinking?

Many people find themselves trapped in a never-ending cycle of frustration and despair as a result of drinking -- feeling bad, feeling sick, feeling embarrassed, feeling ashamed.

If that describes you in any way, I have good news: there is a solution. There is a path out of despair. Drinking no longer has to negatively impact your life or fill you with shame, regret, or those God-awful hangovers.

Millions of us once felt just like you, imprisoned by an addiction that some of us didn't realize we had. Alcoholism is a subtle and sneaky little bastard. It will try to convince you that it's your friend, but will kill you if given a chance. I know this first hand because I spent decades trapped in a repetitive cycle of destructive drinking that almost destroyed my life and nearly killed me several times.

Through the pages of this book, I want to share with you what I went through and what I learned about alcoholism, addiction, recovery, sobriety, and rebuilding a life filled with joy, peace, and purpose. Hopefully, I will dispel some of the mystery that surrounds the process of getting and staying sober.

What is it like getting sober? How do you get sober? What happens in sobriety? Is staying sober difficult? Is it scary, getting sober? How do I socialize without drinking? These are common questions most people have when considering the idea of getting sober or slowing down their drinking. This book will answer many of those questions.

Most importantly, I want to clearly illustrate the *7 Stages* of recovery that I experienced in my sobriety. The *7 Stages* are not the only path to sobriety, nor will they be experienced by everyone in sequential order as I'm presenting them here. However, I have discovered that most people who are successful at getting sober and staying sober, travel a similar road to recovery.

Not everyone's story is identical, but our stories are usually similar concerning the *emotional stages* we pass through in recovery. The details of my story might not be the same as yours. My experience with alcohol might be better, or worse, than your experience. The specifics don't matter. What truly matters is how alcohol impacts our lives. What we're concerned with are the common emotional wounds we all share and hope to repair.

If you've ever thought you might have a drinking

problem (or drug problem) and feel that it's time to get a handle on it, I will share with you everything I've learned during my recovery. I've been sober over twelve years at the time of this writing, and my life post-alcohol is productive, healthy, and exciting. I've found purpose in my life and no longer feel the shame and despair that once dominated my daily existence.

I'm eager to share with you my experience, strength, and hope so that you, too, can find the happiness, health, and joy you deserve. You can do this if you're willing to try!

CONTENTS

DEDICATION	1
WHY YOU MIGHT NEED THIS BOOK	2
WHAT IT WAS LIKE	6
WHAT HAPPENED	9
WHAT TO EXPECT	11
STAGE 1 – DESPAIR	14
STAGE 2 – FEAR	30
STAGE 3 – SORROW	51
STAGE 4 – ACCEPTANCE	69
STAGE 5 – HOPE	91
STAGE 6 – JOY	113
STAGE 7 - PURPOSE	131
WHAT IT'S LIKE NOW	149

WHAT IT WAS LIKE

Addiction is like a dark and gnarled tree that grows from the seed of fear.

I'm convinced that I came out of the womb terrified. That first slap on my ass administered by the doctor was like an alarm clock startling me into a world of anxiety, angst, and fear. I started life afraid of every shadow that crossed my path. It wasn't until I discovered alcohol when I was twelve years old that I was able to suppress the fear, awkwardness, and shyness that dominated me.

In addition to the abundance of fears that plagued me, I was also burdened with an overly sensitive personality. It seemed like everything hurt. Stepping on a bug could make me weep for hours. When I was around five years old, I watched my older brother, Scott, trip while running up a flight of stairs, banging his knee. It didn't seem to bother him very much. He simply stood up and continued on his way with barely a whimper. But I was devastated. The sight of him falling and possibly getting hurt tore me. It was nothing, just a kid falling and jumping back up. But to me, it was excruciating to witness.

Eventually, I began to hate how sensitive I was about every little thing. And I was extremely uncomfortable in the world, an outsider always looking in.

Here, drink this! This will take care of the problem. It's a wonder I waited until I was twelve to start drinking. I got a late start.

I grew up in a small California town that had one movie theater and a pizza parlor. And that was about all there was. It was a quiet place to grow up, dull, and a little boring. My parents divorced when I was three, and my brothers and I were raised by our mom and a father we saw on Saturdays, birthdays, and Christmas. It was a loving family filled with a great deal of humor and laughter. It was also dysfunctional and broken in many ways, like so many other American families.

The first time I remember tasting alcohol was the spoon full of Crème de Menthe my mother allowed me to pour on vanilla ice cream. I don't think it made me feel drunk, but I loved the fact that I was trying something that only adults were allowed to enjoy. It was an innocent gesture on my mom's part, nothing more than adding a little extra sweetener to my dessert. But it made me feel grown-up and cool. Whenever mom wasn't around, I began to add several tablespoons of the sugary liqueur to ice cream, always licking the spoon clean (even at a young age, I instinctively knew that a proper alcoholic never lets a single drop go to waste).

My first "real" drinking experience occurred when the brother of one of my school friends bought us a six-pack of Schlitz Malt Liquor, the extra tall cans. It was a hot, summer day, and we pounded three each in rapid succession. I clearly remember how amazing I felt as soon as the buzz hit me. Warm. Confident. Strong. This was what I had been waiting for my entire life (all 12 years). This was it, the magic potion that would save me. My problems were solved. I was instantly unafraid and courageous. I was invulnerable to harm. The world belonged to me, and I was a king.

The rest of the afternoon was a blur of stumbling, wrestling, laughing, and vomiting. When my mom came home from work, she found her little boy passed out drunk with a layer of puke down the front of his shirt.

The hangover and shame I experienced were awful and humiliating. I promised myself that I would never, ever drink again. Never! Ever! That promise lasted about two weeks.

Over the next 30 years, I continued to chase after that first rush of drunken power. Over the coming decades, I drank, took copious amounts of drugs, and made endless promises to myself that I was never, ever going do it again. Guess how that turned out?

WHAT HAPPENED

The last year of my drinking was a living hell. That may sound dramatic, but there's no other way to describe it. I was 42 years old, flat broke and living alone in a shitty one-bedroom apartment in Los Angeles. I drank every day, snorted and smoked cocaine whenever I could, and hung around other alcoholics and addicts.

I was living a life of quiet desperation. I was a complete mess, physically, mentally, and spiritually. I had been arrested once and had visited the hospital on multiple occasions because of alcohol poisoning and panic attacks. Over the years, I had burned down every meaningful relationship in my life. I was fat, miserable, and lonely. And that's sugar-coating it.

Worst and most destructive of all, I had lost all faith - faith in my abilities, faith in other people, faith in life, faith in any concept of God.

I was drowning in a polluted ocean of addiction and despair. It wasn't until I found the courage to cry out for help that I was saved from the alcoholic destruction that was waiting for me, a form of slow suicide that has killed many of my friends.

The last day I drank was December 8, 2007. The next day, December 9, the gift of desperation descended upon me like a dove. I was extremely hungover, sick, and tired of being sick and tired. I had had enough, and I wanted help. I had tried everything imaginable to get sober on my own, including therapy, acupuncture, and self-will, but nothing worked. It was abundantly clear that I couldn't get sober on my own. I needed help from people who had gone through what I was going through.

I called a friend who was working on his sobriety in Alcoholics Anonymous (AA). He took me to the first of many meetings that I have attended over the last twelve years. I haven't had a drop of alcohol since that first meeting, and I pray every day that I never have another one.

I want to share with you what the experience of getting sober was like - the good, the bad, and the ugly.

WHAT TO EXPECT

As the saying goes, always expect the unexpected. Entering into any new adventure requires an open mind and a willingness to learn and grow.

Getting sober isn't always easy. I'll let you in on a little secret; it can be scary at times, like riding a roller coaster when you're afraid of heights, speed, and loud noises. But it's worth the ride if you're willing to accept that you don't have to be in control. Hold on tight, enjoy the wind in your hair, and see where it takes you. You might be pleasantly surprised.

I want to make it clear that I got sober through the twelve steps of Alcoholics Anonymous. AA is the basis of my sobriety. Therefore it informs my language when I discuss addiction and recovery. AA has saved my life. I love the program and still do my best to practice its principles every day.

But not everyone gets sober this way, and that's fine. There is more than one way to get sober, and I support any method that brings a person lasting peace in recovery.

However, as a "twelve-stepper," I will make references to the steps throughout this book because it is the foundation of my recovery. The steps have been a great road map for me to follow. The point is not to beat you over the head with the steps or explain them in detail. I'm not here to promote the program. I only want to clarify and demystify what it's like to get sober. If you choose AA as a means of getting sober, you will have plenty of time to learn more about each of the twelve steps.

I will often use the word "alcohol" throughout this book. However, the term "alcohol" can be interchangeable with "drugs" or any other destructive substance in your life. Whether you engage in compulsive drug abuse or alcohol abuse, each can be exchanged with the other based on your circumstance.

What I'm attempting to convey in this book are the *stages* most people, myself included, pass through while they're getting sober and cleaning up their life. I've identified *7 Stages* of sobriety and the subsequent emotional experiences you will likely encounter in each stage.

It's important to note that, though you will probably experience each of the *7 Stages* at some point, they might not occur in the exact order that I will present them. For instance, you might experience sorrow (Stage 3) before you experience fear (Stage 2). Or you might feel joy (Stage 6) before hope (Stage 5). It doesn't matter what order they appear, but most likely, you will grapple with each of the 7 Stages at some point.

If you're feeling frightened, angry, or hesitant about giving up alcohol (or drugs), you're not alone. Most people who get sober feel the same way, reluctant to give up the one thing that has given them peace and comfort over the years. But at some point, peace and happiness disappear. Eventually, alcohol mostly brings sadness, regret, and sickness to our lives.

Are you an alcoholic? I have no idea. That's a decision you have to make for yourself. Whatever you decide, getting sober can be accomplished. There is a solution. Millions of people around the world have been successful at achieving lasting peace in recovery. In my own experience, getting sober continues to be the single most significant achievement of my entire life. I love sobriety. Without it, I have nothing, not my health, not my wife, not my home, no money, no serenity, and no hope. Nothing!

As you read through this book, perhaps some of your fear about getting sober will dissipate. You'll discover that there's no mystery to getting sober. It just takes a little hard work, commitment, and a willingness to make some healthy changes that will bring joy and hope back into your life.

If you're willing to try, let's explore what you'll find in the journey ahead.

STAGE 1 – DESPAIR

Life Polluted

Polluted (adjective): made unclean or impure; contaminated; tainted. (Slang): Drunk

Breaking Down

I often wonder if I ever would have bothered getting sober if the physiological results of my drinking hadn't become so brutal. In many ways, it was the physical deterioration I experienced that finally drove me to seek help. Otherwise, I might have just kept going until I dropped dead.

As a teenager and young man, hangovers were barely noticeable. They were minor inconveniences, something to chuckle at proudly, like feeling a bit sore after a tough workout at the gym—no big deal, a slight morning headache and maybe a sour stomach. But certainly nothing close to the skull-crushing, stomach-churning onslaught that alcohol inflicted on my body in middle age.

One of the reasons so many people consider sobriety in their 30s and 40s is that the physical demands of drinking are no longer fun and cute. The older we get, the more brutal and crippling the hangovers become. We lose the ability to deal with the flood of poison we pour into our bodies. And it's important to realize that alcohol is simply that; poison. There is no nutritional value to alcohol. It serves no purpose other than to alter the chemical composition of your brain temporarily.

If you drink long enough and hard enough, your body will begin to rebel against the poison washing through your stomach, liver, and blood. The human body can only take

POLLUTED

so much abuse before it begins to break down from the onslaught. And if like me, you're also adding cigarettes and drugs into the mix, it's only a matter of time before your body collapses from exhaustion.

I first began to notice the extent of my physiological pollution in my late twenties. The hangovers were becoming increasingly intense, like waking up after a night of fistfights, having lost every battle. I felt battered and bruised -- my entire body aching and sore. I started developing terrible, unbearable headaches. I would wake up dizzy and confused. Nausea would overwhelm me, not just in the morning but all day. Eventually, I began to experience intense anxiety and paranoia, along with morning tremors. If you've never experienced alcohol-induced tremors, I can confirm there's nothing quite as disturbing and frightening the first few times they occur. Eventually, I began drinking in the late afternoon just to make the anxiety and shaking subside.

By the time I hit rock bottom, my body was rotting from the inside. My internal organs were no longer functioning correctly. I had fatty liver disease and high blood pressure. I was bloated and looked twenty years older than my actual age. I suffered from constant stomach cramps. I experienced night sweats and intense trembling in my internal organs every morning. My hands shook so badly that it was challenging to sip a cup of coffee.

Over the last few years of my drinking, I had taken myself to the hospital on multiple occasions, thinking I was dying or having a heart attack. I struggled with constant paranoia. I was living through a never-ending cycle of drinking that made me feel horrible twenty-four hours a day, seven days per week.

The worst part of the physical deterioration that many of us experience is that the alcohol we rely on no longer seems to work anymore. For me, this was a terrible and frightening revelation when drinking no longer made me feel better. Drinking started to make me feel worse, both physically and mentally. I would drink more and more, hoping and waiting for the misery to lift, but instead, it just made me feel horrible and sick.

I've spoken to numerous alcoholics over the years that experienced the same phenomenon. The booze simply stops working at some point. Talk about bitter irony! Eventually, the alcohol no longer provides relief and comfort as it did for so many years. Now it just adds to our misery and discomfort. But we keep drinking anyway because we don't know what else to do. We become so enmeshed in relying on this one thing, alcohol, that no other alternative seems possible or achievable.

My body became polluted to the point where I no longer thought I would last much longer. Since those days,

POLLUTED

I have seen many people, including friends I love, reach the same physical state of deterioration. But instead of reaching out for help, they continued on the path they were following, drinking until their bodies simply gave out, sending them to a painful and early grave.

Hope(less)

Without hope, life loses its meaning.

Hope lifts us. Hope gets us out of bed in the morning. Hope allows us to sleep peacefully at night. Hope provides us with anticipation and joy. Hope brings light into darkness. Hope helps us to push forward through difficult times. Hope gives us a desire to grow and improve as we plan for the future.

As soon as we start to feel hopeless, life loses its color and flavor. Depression sets in, and we become cynical and angry. We feel defeated. *What's the point? Who gives a crap?*

Once this started happening, once I began to feel hopeless, I drank MORE in an attempt to recapture the optimism and courage alcohol used to deliver. But my efforts to achieve hope from a bottle were all in vain. The booze no longer worked. I began to spin downward at an accelerated rate of speed. One day bled into the next in a monotonous, boring cycle of drinking, sleeping, eating, drinking, sleeping, eating, drinking. There were days near the end of my three-decade run when I never bothered to get out of bed. I had lost all hope, so why bother getting up and putting on clothes?

It wasn't until I finally got sober that I discovered my need for a belief in something more in life. Up to that point, my concept of God, or a Higher Power, amounted to nothing more than a vague collection of ideas I had collected from books, movies, and the occasional visit to church when I was a child.

It unnerved me to place any faith in something other than my immediate needs and ego. At that stage of my life, my spiritual beliefs were as evolved as a chimp's. Just give me a banana (daiquiri) and leave me alone while I pick my navel and grunt.

There's a reason why alcohol is often called *"spirits."* For many of us, we become spiritually empty to the point where we seek spiritual fulfillment from a bottle.

I believe with all my heart that human beings have an innate need for spiritual nourishment. It's written into our DNA. We need and want a life filled with hope, love, and faith. There is a deep craving within the human soul for more than animal instincts and desires. We must have a spiritual life of some kind, or we remain unfulfilled, often seeking gratification from things that are harmful and destructive. It's particularly true for those of us with addictive personalities. If we don't feel spiritually fulfilled, we destroy ourselves by drinking, snorting, screwing, or eating everything within reach to fill the emptiness gnawing our soul.

Perhaps you know this feeling, too. Maybe you don't feel completely hopeless, not yet. But there might be a desire within you for something more in life, a desire to feed your soul with things more nourishing than alcohol, drugs, or other self-destructive habits.

I was broken down and feeling hopeless. I felt exhausted and sick and wanted relief. Thankfully, the lifeline I was seeking was closer than I realized.

Red Flags

There comes the point if we're lucky when we realize we can't continue living the way we have been. For the most fortunate ones among us, we begin to notice the red flags that keep showing up, clear indicators that something is not right, that maybe it's time to address the problems that always seem to accompany our drinking. For me, countless red flags kept popping up over the years, warning signs I chose to ignore until it was almost too late.

I want to emphasize how lucky you are if you notice these red flags and take them seriously. Sadly, most people choose to ignore the signs, usually ending up with ruined lives, in jail, institutionalized, or dead. It's a statistical fact that the vast majority of alcoholics and addicts in the world never receive the help they need, usually because they choose not to ask for help. Millions of people die as alcoholics and addicts, fully aware of their condition, but too scared to take a leap of faith into recovery.

I put it off as long as I could. I had entirely accepted that I was an alcoholic. I was very aware of this fact in those final years. But it's like knowing you have a serious heart problem, yet choosing not to go to the doctor because you're too frightened to face the treatment that will save you. Confronting and fixing the heart disease is often scarier than admitting you're sick in the first place. Many people just wait for the heart attack to take them out.

The red flags were appearing with higher frequency, and they became impossible to ignore. I was always sick and hungover. I was financially broke and in serious debt. I could never pay bills on time. I had destroyed multiple relationships. I engaged in sexual behavior that was devoid of love or mutual respect. I had lost jobs because of my drinking. I lied to people about my life. I surrounded myself with the dregs of society ("lower companions"), people who were hustlers, drug dealers, and criminals. I had no self-respect. I had developed anxiety and paranoia. I was lonely and afraid.

How many more times could I wake up on the floor of my kitchen, not knowing how I got there? How many more times could I sneak large plastic bags of bottles and cans out of my apartment without my neighbors spotting me? How many more times could I lie to family and friends about the condition of my life? How many more times could I spit in the mirror, disgusted by my reflection?

At some point, we must admit that we've taken it as far as we can, that it's time to change. I knew with absolute certainty that if I continued living this way, I was going to die drunk and alone.

The final year of my drinking was marked by an experience in a motel room when I had drunk myself into an immobile stupor. I was collapsed on the floor and struggling to remain conscious. The amount of alcohol I had consumed was enough to kill a man twice my size. I knew it was unlikely

I would make it through the night.

I was terrified and began to cry out to God for help. I didn't know if I even believed in God, but I was desperate for a life-preserver, and God seemed like the right choice at that moment.

I prayed with everything I had in me, asking for another chance at life. *Please don't let me die like this.*

Miraculously, I survived. When I lifted myself off the floor the next morning, I vowed I would stop drinking.

I didn't keep my vow.

I continued to drink for another year. I tried everything I could to stop on my own, but nothing worked. Filled with shame and guilt, I kept on drinking, no matter how many times I declared NO MORE! The compulsion to drink was just too overpowering, and there didn't seem to be any way of breaking free.

My life in hell, which I had created for myself, continued downward despite the red flags that surrounded me.

Slithering Reptile

I was beginning to sense that I had lost my moral direction in life. In many ways, I had become a liar, a cheater, and a thief.

I never robbed houses. I didn't kill anyone or steal food from orphans. For the most part, I was a nice person, usually polite and friendly. But the painful fact was that I had been living a life filled with immoral behavior for years. I had lied to family and friends about my drinking. I cheated on girlfriends when I was drunk. I took advantage of my employers. I contributed to crime when purchasing street drugs. I endangered the lives of others when I drove drunk. I broke multiple laws when I drove intoxicated or engaged in drug transactions. I surrounded myself with lower companions, criminals, and sociopaths. I disrespected my family by putting my life in danger. I disrespected my body by poisoning it daily. I accumulated debt by spending all my money getting drunk and high. I borrowed money I couldn't repay.

This is just a partial resume, but you get the point.

Somewhere along the journey of my life, I had lost my moral grounding and the willingness to be honest with myself and others. I had slowly, over time, made the decision that the most important thing was having a good time, getting loaded, and neglecting my responsibilities. I dreaded the idea of growing up and becoming a responsible adult, so what better way to prevent that from happening than by staying drunk, foolish, and contemptuous of normal, healthy behavior.

Selfishness is not something we want to admit about ourselves. Nobody wants to admit that they're self-centered, self-serving, or immoral. Not me. Even at my lowest point, I still convinced myself I was a great guy, Mr. Upstanding Citizen.

But the reality, and the truth I had to face, was that I was morally polluted. I had allowed myself to succumb to my lowest impulses. I lived only for pleasure, immediate gratification, and excitement. The realization that I was morally bankrupt was painful to accept, but the truth was impossible to deny. It was one of the lowest, most difficult moments of my life.

I had reached a point when I could no longer stand to look at myself in the mirror. I was ashamed of who I was and what I had allowed myself to become. I was starting to feel like the lowest of creatures, not much more than a slithering reptile whose sole purpose in life was to avoid pain and stay as numb as possible.

I was in desperate need of relief from the way I was living.

Rock Bottom

I had run out of excuses and time. I no longer had the luxury of ignoring the red flags. I had to find a way to clean up my life and get sober, or I was facing a miserable and pathetic death, just another alcoholic who disappears from the radar without a trace. If there was a Bermuda Triangle for alcoholics and addicts, my ship was heading for disaster (I know that's a horrible metaphor, but it makes me laugh, so I'm leaving it in).

I finally hit rock bottom.

Often people hear the term "rock bottom," and they think it means something negative. It certainly sounds negative, the lowest point in a hole where there is nowhere else to go. But if you're an alcoholic who wants to escape addiction, rock bottom is the starting place. Rock bottom means a new beginning for the addict who genuinely wants to get clean and sober. *Rock bottom means rebirth.*

I had reached the stage of my polluted life when I wanted help. It was more than just needing help; I WANTED help. *Enough is enough. Let's fix this shit before it's too late!*

Recalling my vow to God the year before, I fell to my knees on a sunny December day. I was suffering through another horrible hangover when something inside me was triggered to make a sincere cry for help. I went to a local church (I was not a religious person, by any means), and fell to my knees in one of the pews. I prayed with all my mind, body, and soul, pleading for intervention. I needed help and was finally ready to accept it in whatever form it appeared.

There's no other way to explain it but to say something changed in me that day. I left the church and called my friend, Guy, who was already sober. Guy told me to meet him at an AA meeting that night. I promised I would, and this time I kept my promise.

My path to sobriety finally began in earnest. I haven't had a drink in more than 12 years.

My descent to rock bottom took years, and I'm grateful to have survived. But the day I went to my first meeting was only the beginning. I had a long way to go to climb out of the deep hole of addiction, which had left me spiritually and psychologically wounded.

Getting sober and staying sober is not easy. There's no reason to lie about it or make it sound like a picnic filled with cookies and cakes (although there are often some awesome cookies and cakes at AA meetings). The reality of staying sober requires a lot of work. It also demands that we dig deep into our past and find out where things got so screwy, why we do the crazy things we do.

In my journey over the last 12 years, I have come to accept, and embrace, the fact that I'm slightly nuts. I'm incredibly neurotic. I struggle with painful shyness. I'm socially awkward, to the point where I avoid people, especially groups. I'm self-conscious and vain. I often feel entitled and superior to others. I can be incredibly selfish. And I have some, really, really weird shit going on in my head.

But this is just who I am, and I've learned to be comfortable with myself. Through sobriety, I've learned to be happy with who I am, including my nutty mind—learning about ourselves and what makes us tick as human beings are part of the unique and exciting journey of recovery and sobriety.

As I was about to learn, getting, and staying sober wasn't going to be easy. But it sure as hell wasn't going to be boring, either.

Hold on tight, kid. The roller coaster is just getting started.

STAGE 2 – FEAR

Facing the Storm

"Where there is ruin, there is hope for a treasure."

-Rumi

Hands Up

Passing through the doors of that first AA meeting was terrifying. There was a cluster of people lingering near the entrance, chatting and smoking cigarettes (the classic AA cliché). I stood a block away, hiding in the evening shadows, trying to summon the courage to approach. I couldn't move; every bone in my body was telling me to leave. *Just get the hell out of here, go home and have a drink! Who needs this shit! I can get sober on my own! I don't need to be around these weirdos, winos, and bums! It's just a cult! They want to brainwash me! I can do this on my own! Run, motherfucker, run!*

It seems to be a common experience for most people. That first meeting is always insanely frightening. Everyone deals with it in their own way. Some handle it better than others. But all of us enter through those doors for the first time with a level of anxiety boarding on full-blown panic attack.

I smoked one cigarette after another, staring at the entrance to the meeting. Even today, I can remember how badly I was shaking with fear. For a person who had spent the last 32 years trying to drink away fear, I was confronting an epic challenge.

I took a final drag off my cigarette, dropped it on the pavement, and stepped forward toward the door. ***Let's just see what happens.***

"Welcome."

You hear this word a lot in AA meetings. Everyone is always welcoming each other. Welcome. Welcome. Welcome. It's both annoying and sweet, sort of like your mother kissing you as a child; it annoys you, but you don't want her to stop doing it either, even when you're rolling your eyes.

The guy at the front door extended his hand, a big, stupid smile on his face. "Welcome."

I reached out reluctantly to shake his paw. *Why's this asshole so happy?*

That's another thing about meetings. Everyone is always smiling! If you're a frightened, trembling, drunk entering a meeting for the first time, it can really piss you off.

I stepped into the loud, crowded room searching for my friend, Guy. I decided that if I couldn't spot him within thirty seconds, I was leaving. I wanted an excuse to flee.

"Yo, dude! You made it." Guy was standing near a table loaded with snacks and coffee, talking with a small group of people. He waved me over. *Shit, I have no excuse now. I have to stay!*

I approached the group, avoiding eye contact with anyone.

"Welcome," Guy said.

He introduced me to the cluster of people who all repeated the "welcome" mantra while shaking my hand.

I had no idea what to say or do, so I just grinned like an idiot and tried to control my shaking.

As I glanced around the room, I realized there were probably fifty or sixty people there, everyone milling about, drinking coffee, talking loudly, and welcoming each other. Everyone seemed to be in a great mood like they were in a contest to see who could be the happiest. I didn't feel anything close to happy, their joy only serving to darken my mood further. I began to judge every single person in the room, even Guy, for being complete phonies. *No one can be this happy. This is all so fake and contrived! To hell with these toothy clowns!*

After what seemed an eternity, the meeting started when someone began yelling: "Everyone take a seat."

The herd of toothy clowns began jostling for places to sit. Guy pulled me towards two chairs near the center of the room. I was hoping we'd sit in the very back of the room, as far away from everyone as possible. No such luck.

Two people sat at the front of the room, facing the herd. Eventually, I would find out they were the secretary (the person who leads the meeting) and the guest speaker (the person who shares their story).

As the meeting started, the secretary introduced himself as an alcoholic then asked the room: "Are they any other alcoholics present?"

Every hand shot for the sky. A few people even started

POLLUTED

waving their hands in an attempt to draw the room's attention. Look at me! Look at me!

Then the thought crossed my mind; *if I raise my hand, people might look at me.* The secret would be out. They would know. Would they laugh or point? Would they think I was a loser?

My anxiety began to boil over. The shaking in my body increased. *Should I raise my hand? Do I dare admit that I'm an alcoholic in front of a bunch of strangers?* My brain started to work overtime, racing for an answer. *What do I do? What do I do? What do I do?*

It was now or never. It felt like the test of a lifetime, and I was going to fail completely if I didn't raise my hand.

Fuck it!

I slowly raised my hand amongst the forest of hands that surrounded me. No one laughed, stared, or pointed. It only lasted a second, but I felt an enormous wave of energy run through my body, exhilaration, hope, anger, and terror all surging through my veins simultaneously. I didn't realize it at that moment, but by raising my hand and admitting I was an alcoholic, openly and publicly, I was taking the first genuine step forward in recovery. In that split second, I had the opportunity to announce something incredibly painful and scary – I was an alcoholic and needed help.

As I lowered my hand, a single word popped into my head; welcome.

Saint Paul

Many of us have tried to get sober on our own, usually failing miserably. We convince ourselves that if we're just strong enough, or intelligent enough, we can overcome our compulsion to drink. I tried this myself many times. I tried to get sober on my own, so often I lost count. At one point, I even tried acupuncture.

Somehow I convinced myself that if I could just find a wise old Chinese man to stick needles into my body, the obsession to drink would miraculously disappear. I tried it a few times, but sticking needles in me wasn't going to remove over thirty years of addiction and self-destructive impulses. What I truly needed, and what I eventually found in AA, was interaction with other people who were alcoholics just like me, people who understood the insanity of my mind and my deep need to self-medicate.

I first met Paul outside a meeting. I was standing around by myself smoking a cigarette, reluctant and scared to enter the meeting as usual (it took me several months before I was comfortable going to meetings, but I'll get to that later). I was only a few days sober when I saw this stocky, handsome guy with a goatee walking in my direction. The first thing I noticed about him was the way he walked. He had swagger, a cockiness that announced his bravado long before he arrived.

"Hi, I'm Paul. Can I bum one of those?"

I fumbled for a cigarette.

"No problem."

"Going to the meeting?" he asked.

"I think so." I handed him a smoke.

"You think so? Either you are, or you aren't." He said this with a devilish smirk, an expression I was going to become very familiar with over time.

"I guess so. Yes."

He smiled and took a drag off his smoke. He looked like a cat teasing a mouse.

"You new?" he inquired.

"New?"

"To the program?"

"Oh, yes. I'm new. Few days."

"Fantastic!" He seemed genuinely thrilled. That was another weird thing I noticed about people in AA; everyone would get so excited when I told them I was "new," like I had won the lottery, and they were eager to share the spoils.

Paul stuck out his hand like a proud father. I shook it, slightly embarrassed.

"Welcome," he said with that devilish smile. "You're in the right place."

I had no idea why he thought I was in the right place, but he seemed to know what he was talking about, so I just shrugged my shoulders.

"I guess."

"See you inside."

And as quickly as he arrived, he was gone, heading toward the doorway to the meeting.

Over the years, I have often thought that Paul showed up in my life that day for a reason, that some kind of divine energy had coordinated our first encounter. I know that sounds like bullshit, but there's no other way to explain it. He was exactly the person I needed in my life at that moment in time.

I ran into him a few days later, at another meeting. That was the day he became my first sponsor, the person who would lead me through the twelve steps and guide me out of the bitterness, self-loathing, and fear that was at the root of my addiction. I call him Saint Paul because that's what he was to me; an angel and a saint with a goatee, a sly grin, and a huge heart.

Powerless

One of the most terrifying moments of my recovery was admitting that I was powerless over alcohol.

Step One in AA states that we are powerless over alcohol and that our lives have become unmanageable as a direct result of our relationship with alcohol. While I was willing to accept that I drank too much and too often, the idea that I was POWERLESS over alcohol seemed a bit far-fetched.

The word "powerless" implies weakness. Who the hell wants to admit they are weak or dominated by something outside of themselves? Combine that with an over-bloated sense of entitlement and narcissism, asking me to admit that I was powerless over anything felt insulting and demeaning.

How dare you ask me to admit I have no control of something as small and petty as alcohol! Don't you realize how special and remarkable I am? Perhaps I drink too much, maybe way too much. But I'm certainly not powerless over alcohol or anything else! Fuck you.

Paul asked me to write down everything I could remember about my experience with alcohol, the good and the bad -- how it started, how it progressed, and how it ended up. Then I was to write out all the insanity that had occurred over the years and how that insanity led me to seek help.

That night I wrote out my confessional in a torrent of

words that spilled out of me with shocking speed and force. I was amazed at how fast my tale of self-destruction poured out. Once I began to write, it was like a dam breaking. What emerged on those pages was a lifetime of fear and insecurity that I tried to kill with vodka, beer, and wine (and quite a few other things). When I reviewed it, the story seemed bleak and frightening; a sordid tale of debauchery, stupidity, and recklessness.

When it came time for me to read my story back to him, I fully expected Paul to look at me with equal shock and dismay. I was prepared for him to turn away, disgusted by my pathetic excuse of an existence. Indeed, my tale was going to expose me as the lowest form of human excrement that he had ever encountered.

Instead, he listened silently while puffing on a cigar, grinning, and occasionally chuckling at the craziest parts of my story. Otherwise, he remained expressionless.

When I finally finished reading all those many pages to him, Paul said simply:

"Good job."

Good job? That's it? I had spilled my guts out in gory detail. I was expecting something along the lines of: "You sick bastard! Get thee behind me, Satan."

But he didn't seem shocked or disturbed at all. What I would come to learn was that my experience was more typical than unique. I was just another insecure man who turned to alcohol for strength and comfort, but once I took that first drink, all bets were off. I couldn't stop once I started. Alcohol gave me everything I thought I needed, even when it was destroying my life. It turns out I was just another run-of-the-mill drunk, no worse or better than a million other alcoholics stumbling around the planet. I found it strangely comforting to know I was more typical than unique and that maybe I wasn't quite the freak show I assumed I was.

Later that night, having shared my tale with Paul, I felt lighter, less polluted by guilt and shame. A part of me was released. A shift had taken place. For the first time in many years, I slept better than I had in a long time.

Waterworks

I cried so much in those early days that it's difficult remembering what exactly I was crying about all the time. But I definitely cried an awful lot.

It would overwhelm me suddenly, unexpectedly, without warning. I would be watching TV, or taking a walk, or reading a book, or eating an apple, and something would trigger the tears. I would begin to sob, at times uncontrollably, like a child who just saw his puppy get hit by a car.

Now that the numbing agent of alcohol was absent from my life, everything started to rise to the surface unabated. I would be flooded by emotions that I wasn't aware of nor wanted to experience. But they came out, nonetheless, despite my best efforts to control them. Crying became a regular thing for the first few months of my sobriety.

Human beings need to express their emotions. It's as natural as breathing. But as alcoholics, we often choose to suppress unpleasant and painful feelings by drinking them away. Even positive emotions like joy, excitement, and love can often feel prickly and overwhelming. They sting too much. Drinking away positive emotions is as common as drinking away bad ones. Either way, we prefer to remain as numb as possible, lest we feel too much. Why feel anything if we can just open a bottle and feel nothing?

I was frightened by the constant feelings that

POLLUTED

bombarded me like I was under siege. It never seemed to end. One moment I'd be calm and laughing; seconds later, I'd be weeping like a baby. It was weird and sort of pathetic.

I remember watching a movie one night in my apartment. The film was "Sister Act" with Whoopi Goldberg and Maggie Smith. At one point, Maggie Smith's character says to Whoopi's character, "God has brought you here – take the hint."

That was all it took. The flood gates opened. In that single line, I felt like I was receiving a message about my own life: *God has brought you here (to sobriety), so don't fuck it up like everything else in your life.*

I began to sob and weep uncontrollably. I couldn't contain it. I'm watching a comedy and bawling my eyes out like an infant.

And in a way, that's what I was – an infant. I was so new to the concept of feelings and emotions that I was unable to process them in a reasonable manner. Crying just became a part of my day, often several times per day.

It took me a long time to learn how to process my emotions like a healthy adult (several years, in fact). I will never be an altogether "normal" person when it comes to emotions. Emotions still scare me. But one thing I learned in those early days of recovery was that emotions are simply a part of being alive. Running from them, numbing them, drinking them away, is never going to make them disappear. At most, emotions and feelings go dormant for a while. But at some point, they always rise back to the surface. It's best if I just meet them head-on and deal with them then and there, as soon as they appear.

One thing I learned to appreciate about AA meetings is that people are so damn willing and eager to share their emotions with others, out loud and proud for the whole world to see and hear. People laugh as readily as they cry in meetings. It was strange as hell at first, but over time I got used to being around people expressing themselves openly in meetings. Eventually, I got comfortable enough to do the same thing, too.

I was still a long way from opening up too much in front of other people, but I was starting to tap into something deeper within me that was struggling to get out.

Night Creatures

During those early months, the biggest challenge for me was the loneliness, boredom, and fear that descended upon me as soon as it started getting dark. The nights were the toughest part of the journey when I first got sober because I did the majority of my drinking at night.

I would usually start my first drink around 5:00 pm and continue drinking until I either: A) ran out of booze, B) ran out of money, or C) passed out.

It wasn't until I stopped drinking that I realized I was... *afraid of the dark.*

When we say someone is afraid of the dark, usually we think of a small child frightened by monsters under the bed or in the closet waiting to attack. It's not a term we typically assign to adults. But there I was, a grown man afraid of the dark. The only difference was that the closet where the monsters were hiding was my head. What I discovered was that my brain was crowded with monsters, goblins, and beasts that were eager to attack me at every opportunity. My head was swarming with night creatures that were continually telling me what a piece of shit loser I was, that the only way I was going to feel better was to take a drink. The monsters in my head were hungry, and they fed on fear and loneliness.

Not giving in to temptation was brutal. I would be at home watching TV, fidgeting and anxious when someone in a show would pour themselves a scotch. Just the sound of the ice clinking on the side of the glass could send me into a frenzy of obsession. My head would spin. I wanted to lick the television screen. The monsters in my head would start to claw and bite, demanding that I head immediately to the liquor store to quench my thirst.

Those were the toughest hours of my early sobriety, the nights. I was so accustomed to drinking myself into oblivion every night that I no longer knew what to do once the sun went down.

Over time I developed a few positive habits that kept me from drinking:

- Call a sober friend
- Go to an AA meeting
- Read addiction books
- Take a long walk
- Ride my bike
- Eat ice cream

There were several months when I would eat a pint of ice cream every night. I gained a bit of weight, but I didn't drink, and that's all that mattered. I figured I could lose the weight later. I was willing to do whatever it took not to pick up that first drink.

Sleeping came in fits and starts. Rarely did I enjoy

a full night of peaceful rest. My dreams were strange and frightening. I woke up frequently, often drenched in sweat. Yet I somehow managed to push through night after night, waiting for the sun to rise the next day, eager to start over fresh and *still sober.*

In AA, they say we stay sober one day at a time. In those early days, one night at a time was the toughest part.

Fighting Through

Sooner or later, we all have to make the decision; do I stay sober and clean, or do I allow alcohol to pollute my life and control me? Do I fight or do I crumble in defeat?

I was still completely obsessed with alcohol. I never stopped thinking about it or craving it. Even though I was fully aware of how destructive it was for me, I continually told myself how easy it would be to have *just one* drink. No one would know. No one would care. *Just one,* and I'll feel better instantly. *Just one* and all my problems will go away. *Just one* and I'll be able to sleep. *Just one* and the fear will subside. *Just one* and the monsters in my head will hibernate.

The obsession to drink was overwhelming and dominated every aspect of my existence. The simple act of walking through a grocery store was like navigating a battlefield. Passing the liquor aisle was treacherous and terrifying, forcing me to avert my eyes away from the army of glimmering bottles towering over my head.

I would think about drinking all day long. I dreamed about drinking every night (twelve years sober, and I still dream about drinking occasionally, but it doesn't bother me anymore).

Going to a restaurant that served alcohol was torturous. If someone were drinking a glass of wine at a table near me, I would stare at it impulsively, watching every sip they

POLLUTED

took, wondering how it tasted and fantasizing about how it was making them feel. I sexualized alcohol, romanticized it, desiring it with deep longing.

Alcohol occupies an enormous space in western culture. Everywhere you turn, there it is. There's a bar or restaurant serving booze on every block. Even movie theaters sell beer and wine these days. There's no getting away from it; this is just a fact and something we have to face and work through if we want to stay clean.

Finally, the fear I had been wallowing in for so long began to transition into anger. Instead of feeling afraid at everybody and everything, I became increasingly pissed off and frustrated.

Why the fuck do I have to feel like this all the time?

Why the fuck am I controlled by a liquid?

Why the fuck am I so afraid of life?

Why the fuck am I so afraid of people?

Why the fuck?

Why the fuck?

Why the fuck?

The anger finally boiled over in a meeting. I was never one to raise my hand or share in AA meetings. I preferred to hide out in the back of the room and listen without speaking. But one day, while sitting silently in the back of the room, I let loose. I had had enough and needed to vent my rage and frustration. I had no idea what I wanted to say, but I had to speak. I had to release my feelings, or they were going to kill me.

I thrust my hand skyward. I hated speaking in public (still do). My face flushed with blood as soon as the secretary pointed to me. Everyone in the room turned their gaze in my direction. It's now or never.

"My name is Dirk, and I'm an alcoholic."

A loud chorus of "*Hi, Dirk*" filled the room.

"I can't handle this shit." My voice was trembling. "It feels like there's something trapped inside me, an animal. It's eating me alive. I want to feel better. I want to stop obsessing over alcohol all the time. I feel like I'm losing my mind..."

I ranted and raved for about five minutes. I'm sure I didn't make much sense. There wasn't any forethought or a coherent message. The words poured out of me in a toxic deluge. Everyone in the meeting just smiled and nodded like they understood everything I was saying. And in a way they did. Perhaps the words didn't make sense, but the emotions were evident. It was my turn to unleash the storm of feelings and fear that had been building inside me for so long.

When it was over, I just said, "Thanks for listening," and everyone applauded enthusiastically.

When I finished, I was drained of emotion, shaking and

POLLUTED

dripping with sweat. It reminded me of the day in the church when I had cried out to God for help. By speaking out loud and sharing my story, however incoherent and insane it probably sounded, something had changed in me. That was the day I began to recognize that there was anger in me that I could use to my benefit. Anger, I realized, could be a gift, a way to express myself and break free from the fear and anxiety that imprisoned me.

Anger might not always be a healthy form of expression, but if it could help me fight through my fear and keep me from drinking, then I would use it!

I was angry, damn it, and ready to do whatever was necessary to stay sober.

STAGE 3 – SORROW
What Have I Done?

"Every man has his secret sorrows which the world knows not; and often times we call a man cold when he is only sad."

-Henry Wadsworth Longfellow

POLLUTED

Regret

I found it incredibly difficult to let go of the past. I spent most of my waking hours thinking about what was and what could have been. Why did things turn out the way they did? Why did I make certain decisions? Why did I let this person into my life? Why did I hurt someone I loved? Why did they hurt me? Why did I spend so much time in self-destructive pursuits? Why didn't I pay more attention to the red flags when they first appeared?

The list of regrets was endless and haunted me day and night.

A big part of recovery for me was the sorrow I felt because of the poor decisions I had made and the lifestyle I had pursued. It made me sad and angry to think about *"what could've been"* and the potential I had sacrificed in aimless pursuits. It wasn't supposed to turn out this way. My life was supposed to be epic and triumphant, not small and broken. By this stage in my life, I was *supposed* to have all the cash and prizes. I was *supposed* to be one of the winners. I was *supposed* to have a fat bank account. I was *supposed* to have a big house. I was *supposed* to have a wife and children. I was *supposed* to have fame, fortune, and adulation.

Instead, I had sickness, debt, and regret. Oops. Sometimes the best-laid plans of mice and men can turn into a steaming pile of shit.

Looking back, I was shocked by the number of bad decisions I had made during my life. Red flags aside, I had made most of my choices over the years based entirely on immediate gratification. I wanted to feel good, and I wanted to feel good now! I always seemed to be seeking instant happiness and euphoria in every aspect of my life, including work, family, romance, and finance. The most consistent and recurring element of my time on earth was the drinking I did in an attempt to find serenity and joy. Why try to accomplishing anything substantial when I can just drink six beers and feel like I run the world?

The wreckage of my past was not a pretty sight to behold. But it was something I had to face to move forward. I had to look back and fully embrace all the mistakes and bad decisions I had made in my life, and be willing to forgive myself and others who had hurt me. Otherwise, I was doomed to repeat the past and keep swallowing the poison of regret that polluted my mind and soul.

Like Dogs

As I continued to review my past mistakes and flawed decisions, it occurred to me that I had also made some horrible choices when it came to people I associated with over the years. I had gravitated towards people who were like me – alcoholics and addicts.

Whenever I take our dog for a walk, the second she spots another dog, even blocks away, she freezes in her tracks and stares. The other dog usually does the same thing. Then the inevitable tug of war takes place as each dog strains against its leash to greet one other and start the ass-smelling ritual.

This is how alcoholics and addicts seem to find each other, too. We can enter a room, party, or office and be drawn to one another like dogs (hopefully without the ass-smelling, but not always). There is an unconscious pull that brings us together.

Once we meet and establish a friendship or relationship, we provide cover for one another in our behavior and habits.

These friendships always start fun and exciting. We've found someone who likes to drink as much as we do. *Woo hoo!* As long as we stick together, our lifestyle and hangovers start to seem normal. *This is how everyone behaves, right?*

As I looked backward, it dawned on me that my life was populated by people who were as equally fucked-up as me. Most of them were kind, funny, and smart. Many were brilliant, ambitious, and financially successful. Many owned businesses and were raising families. There were writers, actors, and even a few doctors. I have snorted cocaine with an anesthesiologist and a police officer. They were black, white, Asian, and Hispanic; men, women, gay, straight, and everything in between.

One thing that is certain about addiction; it doesn't discriminate across race, gender, class, or social status. It's an equal-opportunity disease that welcomes everyone into its home. Everyone is invited.

My first instinct was to blame the people who had come in and out of my life. I wanted to point the finger at everyone else and say IT WAS YOUR FAULT! YOU DID THIS TO ME! I was angry and sad about some of the friendships I had developed over the years. *Who are these people and how the hell did I end up with them?*

It took me a long time to fully realize that the people I had surrounded myself with were often just as sick as I was. Many of them were alcoholics and addicts who were searching for comfort and meaning in the world. Somehow, we found each other and took the journey together into the realms of self-destruction and addiction.

Sadly, and inevitably, a number of those people never made it out. Many died along the way. Even today, twelve years into my sobriety, I occasionally get a call or email informing me of an old friend who succumbed to their addictions and died sad, lonely, and broken. One of my closest friends, Eric, from my drinking days, just died recently from an overdose. He tried to get sober for years, but just couldn't make it work for whatever reason. Eric was a good man, brilliant and kind. But his addictions were more powerful than he ever realized, and they took him out before he could escape his demons.

One of the great things about AA and something I cherish to this day is that I began to meet people who were trying to improve their lives by getting clean and healthy. I was now surrounded by the survivors who were after the same thing I was – a life free from addiction and filled with possibility and hope. We were still dogs sniffing each other out, but now our common bond was a desire to **STOP** drinking, not a compulsion to **KEEP** drinking. *Woof woof.*

Waves

I first started experiencing depression when I was around 14 years old. It would hit me in violent waves, without warning. I never knew when it was coming, how long it would last, or how far down it would take me. I could never figure out what triggered the episodes, so I had no way of avoiding them. My mood would shift with startling speed into a dark hole of sadness. I would become overwhelmed by a thick, heavy feeling of hopelessness, a sense that there was no meaning to life, or that I had any purpose on earth. I was a useless piece of shit, and death felt like the only escape.

Perhaps I could've received the help I needed through professional counseling, but I never bothered to tell my parents or anyone else, so it remained untreated for many years. However, I discovered quickly that Dr. Budweiser was a very competent therapist who provided me with an instant fix to my problems. A six-pack therapy session only cost around $5 in those days, not a bad deal and an easy way to kick the blues. Bottoms up!

Teenage angst is certainly not uncommon. It's no surprise that kids have been turning to alcohol and drugs for decades to make it through their high school years when their hormones and emotions are waging war on their young brains. The waves of depression I experienced were crushing. The only way I got through those periods was by self-medicating with a steady stream of drinking.

POLLUTED

I have often said to other alcoholics that I don't think I could've survived growing up had I not been able to drink through the depressions. Ironically, booze saved me before it almost killed me.

The collapse was inevitable. I had been regulating my feelings with booze for so long that my ability to control my emotions was almost non-existent once I finally got sober. It was just like being a teenager all over again, only an older, fatter version. The waves would crash down on me with horrendous force, leaving me dazed and sometimes unable to get out of bed.

I often wanted to return to the bottle for relief. I would be at home, doing nothing but lying in bed watching TV for days on end, never leaving my apartment. I wanted to drink, but I didn't want to drink. I knew I needed to go to a meeting, but at that stage, I still hated going to meetings (that would change later). I knew I should call Paul for advice, but I hated the idea of asking another dude for help all the time (so *"unmanly,"* I thought). I should leave my apartment, go outside for fresh air, but the idea of hearing birds and feeling sunlight repulsed me.

Eventually, the depression would lift. Sometimes it would last only a few hours, sometimes several days. Once I was able to crawl out of bed, I knew what I had to do:

1. Call Paul
2. Go to a meeting

Paul was extremely patient with my mood swings and outbursts. There were times I would call him and blubber and sob uncontrollably about whatever was bothering me that minute. I cried like a baby or ranted like a maniac. Either way, he remained calm and steady. As I said, the man was a saint.

One of the most challenging and dangerous stages of early sobriety is the inevitable crash that comes. It seems to happen to most people I've met in recovery. We all go through a period of intense sadness and sorrow as we begin to rebuild and repair our lives. For the first time, perhaps ever, we're learning how to absorb and process emotions, anger, and depression without the aid and comfort that booze used to bring us. We're learning how to deal with *life on life's terms*. It's a hazardous period, and many people don't make it through without going back to the bottle.

Over the last 12 years, I've learned to cope with my depression in healthy and productive ways. It never went away entirely. I have accepted the fact that I am always going to experience bouts of depression. But how I handle these episodes has changed dramatically. Exercise, meditation, prayer, or meetings are usually all I need to lift myself out of the dark hole. I've learned to identify their arrival early and can fix the problem before it overwhelms me.

But in those early days of my recovery, the waves were brutal and frightening. Thankfully, between Paul and the meetings I attended, I survived without visiting Dr. Budweiser.

Sick Tomato

I still have my old driver's license from my last year of drinking. Occasionally, I pull it out from my sock drawer to look at it as a reminder.

In the photograph, my usually narrow face is round and red with a thick double chin. My hair, which has always been close to blonde, is dark, greasy, and looks like I cut it myself with a fork and knife. I look pissed off in the photo, lips narrowed, eyes squinting. There is zero joy in my face. I look like an angry tomato.

Years of booze-guzzling, coke-snorting, and cigarette-inhaling had taken their toll (shocker!). As I mentioned earlier, during the final stretch of my drinking, I was in dangerously bad shape. My body was starting to give up on me. My doctor informed me that I had a fatty liver, high blood pressure, and elevated cholesterol levels. My skin, hair, and teeth were showing signs of early decay. I was grossly overweight and could barely walk up a flight of stairs without stopping to gasp.

Alcohol is one of the worst things we can put into our system. It wreaks havoc. There's not a single thing in alcohol your body needs or wants. It's poison when consumed in large enough quantities over a long enough period of time.

In the early days of my new sobriety, I could hardly sleep and would often break out in cold sweat as my body worked to squeeze out all the toxins that had pooled in every pore. I would sweat so much at night that I had to keep buying new pillowcases to replace the ones that were stained yellow. My skin was blotchy and dry. My heart would race so fast it felt like it would explode. I suffered from anxiety and paranoia. My stomach was in constant agony. I had horrible pain and discomfort in my belly morning, noon, and night. There were times that it was almost unbearable. I would curl up on my couch and moan from the pain. And the farting! It sounded like a fog horn was lodged up my ass. The windows rattled at times. Of course, being a hypochondriac, I was convinced that the pain was caused by stomach cancer and that I would die soon.

My physical condition deepened the depression I was experiencing at the time. I became despondent, wondering if I would ever feel half-way normal again.

I have always been vain, and it made me sad to think I had inflicted so much damage to my body. I felt and looked like shit. My body was trying to repair itself, and it was taking longer than I could've anticipated.

There were brief moments when I would feel great, especially after the first few weeks of not drinking. Waking up without hangovers was like a miracle. The morning shakes were fading. And the nausea that had become routine was no longer a constant presence. But my body was made weak by long-term substance abuse, and I never seemed to feel completely well.

Eventually, I learned that if I took a few walks every day, I would begin to feel better. And I made a concerted effort to improve my diet. I had been living on booze, cheeseburgers, and top ramen for a long time, and the results were noticeable. I started to increase my consumption of fruits and vegetables and make healthier choices in what I ate each day.

Progress was slow. Yet over time, my body began to heal and repair itself. Whenever I was feeling particularly low or unmotivated, all I had to do was pull out my driver's license to get a quick reminder of where I had been just a short time earlier — a sick, angry, flatulent tomato.

Heart Matters

When I first got sober, I spent a lot of time thinking about the numerous mistakes of my life. Where did it all go wrong? How did I fuck things up so badly?

Reviewing the wreckage of my past, I noticed a recurring issue that appeared throughout my life – terrible relationships. In terms of dating and romance, my past looked like a graveyard.

All of the relationships I had been in were started either at bars or parties, fueled by cocktails. It was astonishing to realize that I couldn't identify a single one that hadn't involved alcohol from the outset.

They were all doomed from the start. My romantic past ("romantic" haha) was nothing but a long string of drinking-friends-with-benefits, notable mostly for constant fighting and painful breakups. Each of these relationships started out fun and exciting, but quickly dissolved into insults, manipulation, cheating and screaming, *lots and lots of screaming*. All these years later, my ears are still ringing.

I assumed I would never experience a calm, peaceful relationship built on mutual respect and trust.

I think most alcoholics and addicts seek out drama in relationships. We get high from the adrenaline created by chaos and pain. We crave lives filled with euphoria, followed by depression. Up and down! High and low! Around and

POLLUTED

around we go. As long as we keep living in the tornado, we never realize the destruction we're creating.

As I started working on my sobriety, I began to review a lifetime of broken relationships. It was a pathetic view to behold. Like many people, alcoholic or not, I had clung to the idea that if I could just find the right person – The One – then all my problems would be solved. I wouldn't have any more worries. My existence on earth would finally matter once I found the perfect mate or spouse. The love of another person would validate me.

It had never dawned on me that to be in a healthy, loving relationship, I needed to be a healthy, caring person instead of a raging, self-centered alcoholic. *Now there's a novel concept.*

It took a long time to realize that the search for The One who could save me was futile and pointless. Seeking validation from another person was no different than seeking comfort from a bottle of vodka. I was searching outside for something that needed to be fixed inside. Until I could find validation and happiness from within, I was doomed to keep repeating the same patterns in every part of my life.

I was filled with resentment and sorrow for the past I had created. I wanted relief for the pain in my heart, the emptiness that seemed to follow me everywhere I went.

Resentment

There is a saying that I learned early in recovery: *resentment is like swallowing poison and waiting for the other person to die.*

One of the most important things I came to realize in the initial stages of my sobriety was that I had accumulated an enormous amount of resentment towards the people in my life, past, and present. Whether it was friends, girlfriends, employers, family members, or the local coffee shop barista, I had recorded and retained every insult, betrayal, and slight that had ever occurred over my lifetime. I wanted to blame everyone I had ever encountered for everything that had gone wrong in my life. *I'm not to blame, you are!*

I held on to resentment and self-pity like a shield, a way to deflect personal responsibility for my actions. But the truth was, I had been swallowing as much resentment as booze over the years, and both had been poisoning me.

Step Four in AA is known as the resentment step. Step Four is our opportunity to identify the source of our pain, anger, fear, and all the other negative emotions that rule our lives. To put it in poetic terms, *this is where the shit hits the fan.*

A lot of people are terrified of this step. It requires that we write down every single thing that has pissed us off or hurt our feelings, EVER! I don't mean just in the last few months.

POLLUTED

I mean, EVER! Childhood, school, birthday parties, dates, jobs, drug deals, family vacations, etc. every moment of your life needs to be recorded and reviewed if it involved pain, sadness, anger, or fear. Was your pride hurt? Did it damage your self-esteem? Did it make you feel deprived, despised, or unloved? Find it and write it down.

When Paul instructed me how to proceed, it seemed like a monumental task. How the hell was I supposed to remember EVERYTHING and EVERYBODY that ever hurt me in any way? I was reluctant to begin and thought it sounded like an epic joke.

But once I started writing, it seemed effortless! I filled page after page of perceived wrongs that had been inflicted upon me. I had no idea that there was so much waiting to come out. I found myself writing down the names and pain caused by every schoolyard bully, teacher, girlfriend, employer, friend, family member, or stranger who had ever inflicted the slightest damage to my precious little ego. I had no idea, until it was all out on paper, how much resentment I had stored up and saved over the decades.

I worked on it for days, and when I finally felt I had unearthed every detail, I had to read it back to Paul.

Again, his reaction was pretty much the same as when I read him my history of drinking. No shock or horror, just a paternal "good job," then on to the next thing.

But it was an eye-opening experience. Most importantly, it initiated an opportunity for forgiveness. If resentment is the poison, then forgiveness is the antidote.

Facing pain and resentment is one of the most challenging things we can do, whether we're alcoholics or not. Paul informed me that if I wanted relief from the poison of resentment, I would have to learn how to forgive others, no matter what. Someone broke my heart: forgive. Someone fired me from a job: forgive. Someone stole from me: forgive. Someone tried to ruin my life: forgive. Forgive. Forgive. Forgive.

Not a simple thing to ask of a half-demented man-child who was struggling daily not to drink. I began to review my resentments, looking for a way to forgive everyone on the list.

What became apparent was *my part* in every situation. As I began the process of forgiving others, I began to realize that I had played a role in every single incident. It takes two to tango, right? Why was I there in the first place? How did my actions possibly hurt the other person? What could I have done differently? Could I have been more sensitive or loving? Was I at fault sometimes?

It was a strange and liberating experience, learning how to forgive and see my part in each situation. Not easy, but illuminating. For the first time, I started seeing the world, and my place in it, much differently. This was a big step forward in personal responsibility, never my favorite topic, but necessary if I wanted to heal.

    Something within me was starting to change. Much of my anger and fear began to slowly dissolve as I continued to forgive everyone on my list. For the first time, I was starting to feel slightly better, like I could breathe again.

STAGE 4 – ACCEPTANCE

Maybe I Belong Here

"The worst loneliness is to not be comfortable with yourself."

-Mark Twain

Pink Clouds

At one point or another, almost every alcoholic passes through a pink cloud phase of their recovery. For some people, it starts after a few days or weeks of sobriety. For others, it kicks in after a few months. But no matter when it occurs, it seems to be a universal experience that can be both exhilarating and dangerous.

The most accurate way to define the pink cloud is "false euphoria" or "synthetic bliss." This is the time when our heads begin to clear, we're getting more rest, our senses are reawakening, and we feel like we're floating on fluffy pink clouds of joy and happiness.

It brings a fantastic sense of optimism and hope because we finally feel like we're free and clear from the chains of our addiction that held us captive for so long. We start to think: *I'm good. There's nothing to worry about here. I've got this. I'm in the clear now.*

One of the things I noticed the most in my pink cloud phase was how good everything smelled. It was strange. It seemed like I could smell everything in the world, and each aroma brought a flood of pleasant emotions and memories to my mind. A specific type of flower would remind me of my grandmother. Freshly cut grass brought back fond memories of my childhood. It felt like I was sharply attuned to all the intricate details of the world, and that I would live in peace and joy for the rest of my life.

Ironically, the pink cloud phase of recovery is very similar to the experience of snorting cocaine. We snort the first line, and there's the rapid upward swing of exhilaration when the world seems magnificent. Then there's the inevitable crash as the blow runs out. We fall rapidly from a pink cloud of bliss to the brown mud of depression.

The pink cloud in recovery can be similar. One moment we're floating on a cloud of optimism and hope; the next moment, we descend into depression, irritability, and frustration.

Early recovery for me was filled with peaks and valleys. I would be on top of the world one day, and the next day I'd be drowning in misery. It sucked and left me confused and desperate for emotional consistency.

There was a constant war raging inside me; do I stay sober and fight through the emotional swings, or do I take the easier way out and pick up a drink. *Stay sober or drink? Stay sober or drink? Stay sober or drink?*

I realized early on that if I could just manage to make it to a meeting every day, my chance of surviving twenty-four hours without drinking increased exponentially. Something about AA meetings seemed to resonate with me. I still didn't WANT to go to meetings or particularly enjoy them. But every single time I went to a meeting, especially at night, the urge to drink went away almost entirely. Was it the stories I was hearing people share? Was it the prayers they were always reciting? Was it the fucking hand-holding at the conclusion of each meeting (I hated that part)? What was it that left me feeling better after each meeting? What was it about the meetings that diminished my urge to drink?

Honestly, 12 years later, I still don't know the answers to these questions (I don't mind the hand-holding anymore, either). What I learned early in my recovery was that if I could just make it to a meeting every day, I might survive without picking up a drink. And that's all I wanted. I didn't care about anything else, not the prayers or the hand-holding, nor my mood swings or depressions. I only cared about one thing: NOT DRINKING!

The pink clouds came and went. My emotions went up and down all the time, an endless rollercoaster of highs and lows, euphoria, and angst. But I kept going to meetings because I knew that's where I needed to be.

Eye Contact

I've always been a blusher. Since childhood, I've experienced a maddening rush of blood to my face whenever I feel awkward or embarrassed. The most frustrating part about being a blusher is that when I blush, I become *more* embarrassed by people *knowing* I'm blushing, which then makes me blush even harder. When the blushing increases, the blood rushes into my ears, making it difficult to hear. Once my face flushes hot, and my hearing is impaired, I become confused and begin to stammer and stutter. It's a vicious cycle of humiliation that I've struggled with ever since I can remember.

Over time, I worked hard to avoid any type of situation that might embarrass me. Socializing in large groups, approaching a girl I liked, speaking out loud, attending parties, dancing, all made me feel incredibly uncomfortable and awkward.

Booze changed everything for me.

I realized early in life that many situations that induced embarrassment could be easily conquered with a few drinks. By my teens, I rarely engaged in any type of social activity without downing a few beers whenever possible. Drinking gave me the courage to look people in the eye, speak out loud, joke, dance, and, most importantly, talk to girls.

By the time I got sober, I was almost entirely clueless

POLLUTED

when it came to socializing without liquid courage. It felt like I was starting all over again, reverting to my childhood when I blushed and stammered so often. It was awful, and left me feeling discouraged. *Who the hell wants to revisit the most painful parts of their childhood?*

In many ways, getting sober is about starting over from the place where it all began. If I began drinking at age 12, then that's when I stopped maturing in certain parts of my life. Essentially, I stopped growing up at age 12. Now at age 43, I was being forced to return to the starting gate, relearning what I had tried to escape through alcohol.

The early stages of my recovery included a lot of blushing and stammering.

It was discouraging to realize that I was unable to look people in the eyes without turning my gaze away, my cheeks flushing beet red, words getting stuck in my throat. Trying to talk out loud and engage in eye contact felt unbearable at times.

When I attended AA meetings, I would show up late to avoid talking with anyone. I would sit in the back of the room whenever possible. As soon as the meeting ended, I'd race for the door and disappear lest I have to engage in any conversation.

But I kept showing up anyway. The way I figured it, showing up was 90% of the battle. So what if I didn't talk with anyone? I was there to listen, and that's what I needed at that stage.

What I noticed was that the more I attended meetings, the more I began to recognize people. They, in turn, began to recognize me. A few people even knew my name. That was huge. They would shake my hand (or, God forbid, hug me) and say, "Hi, Dirk. Welcome back," like I was a long lost relative. At first, it freaked me out, but then I started to enjoy it, and to look forward to hearing my name welcoming me into the meetings (*I'll let you in on a little secret; I even started to look forward to the occasional hug. Shhh, don't tell anyone*).

It was a small event when it happened, but it felt good to be recognized and acknowledged. I began to crave those small intimate interactions at the meetings when people would say hello and say my name out loud.

The big break-through for me was when someone asked me to stand by the door of a meeting I attended every Sunday to be a "greeter." A greeter is just someone who stands there and says "welcome" to every person that passes through the door.

So instead of being the terrified newcomer, I was now going to be the grinning idiot who said "welcome" to everyone.

This was a pivotal and positive turning point in my recovery.

POLLUTED

At first, I blushed and stammered when I greeted people, feeling like a complete phony and fool. Surely, all these people would know I was new to this whole sobriety thing and laugh at me or talk about me behind my back. What right did I have to be a greeter at a meeting? I was nobody; I meant nothing. They would probably insist I be kicked out of the meeting forever.

It made me nervous as hell to be a greeter when I first started. But then I began to enjoy it. Every Sunday, I'd arrive at the meeting early and begin the process of saying "welcome" and shaking hands with everyone as they passed through the doors. I even started trying to figure out who was brand new and terrified like I had been at my first meeting. When I would spot one of these trembling newcomers (they often look like Bambi in the headlights), I would greet them extra warmly and sometimes rub their arm in a gesture of solidarity.

What the hell was going on? I was having a good time on Sundays because I could be a greeter. I was able to shake people's hands, say "welcome" and look them in the eye... WITHOUT BLUSHING!

What the fuck is happening here?

Compadres

The progression was natural. The more meetings I attended, the more likely I would start to recognize people, and they would recognize me in turn. Eventually, if I could somehow overcome my intense shyness, a few conversations would arise, and before I knew it, a friendship might develop, a friendship born in sobriety.

Starting a friendship in sobriety is different than starting one in addiction. As fellow alcoholics in recovery, we're drawn together by shared adversity and pain. The bonds formed in the early days of recovery are often intense and long-lasting, similar to soldiers who fought in the same war. There is a shared understanding and honesty between the combatants that other people, outside the sacred circle, simply can't understand.

Being a greeter every Sunday had a tremendous impact on my confidence. It seems silly that the simple act of welcoming people into a meeting could improve my self-esteem. Yet, I was at such a low emotional state when I started my sobriety that this weekly ritual had a significant effect on my ability, and willingness, to start talking with people before and after meetings. Over a few weeks, I began to know many people in the meetings, some who would eventually become close friends.

I've always had a difficult time being around other

human beings and developing friendships. When I'm not emboldened with booze, people make me feel nervous and inadequate. I don't mean people who are assholes either. I mean ordinary, kind, funny, decent people. There's always been something inside me that makes me feel "*less than*" others as if everyone is somehow better than me. I've always felt like an outsider, an uninvited guest who is loitering at the secret social club of life. While everyone is inside having a party, I'm stuck on the outside peeking through the window, hoping that someday I'll be asked to join the festivities.

For the first time in my life, I began to feel like I BELONGED somewhere. Being a part of AA started to feel like I had come home. I still didn't want to go to meetings, but I began to realize that these were *my* people. This nutty flock of drunks and addicts were my compadres. Here was my fiesta. Here was the party I had been waiting to join, and I was invited inside, no questions asked. Granted, the party had no booze or blow, but still...

One of the first friendships I developed in AA was with Dave W., one of the funniest people I ever met in my life. Dave and I would sit next to each other in meetings (we both got sober around the same time) and laugh like a couple of school girls at all the crazy shit going on around us in those meetings.

Every time I spotted Dave at a meeting, I moved quickly to find a seat next to him. He could be moody as hell, but never disappointed when it came to making me laugh. With his subtle, southern drawl and world-weary attitude, he was the companion I needed in those early, shaky days. Five years later, Dave would be at my wedding, a bright and sober compadre that I'm forever grateful to call a friend.

Making new friends felt like an accomplishment, something I was enjoying every day. I was still struggling with shyness (even to this day), but my life felt like it was expanding in a positive direction. I still had a lot to face in the journey ahead, and depression and fear were a big part of my daily existence. But I was finally starting to meet people just like me who were lost, vulnerable and lonely. All of us broken soldiers trying to pick up the pieces of their shattered lives together.

Until You Want To

For a long time, going to AA meetings was usually accompanied by dread. I simply didn't want to go. Even though I knew I needed to be there, I still suffered from intense social anxiety. It didn't matter that it was a gathering of fellow drunks like me or that I was starting to make new friends. It was still a *group of people*, which always made me feel shy and agitated.

In those early days, I tried to go to a meeting every day, and every day I tried to talk myself out of going. I came up with an endless list of excuses why I didn't want to go or need to go to a meeting:

Meetings are bullshit!

Meetings are boring!

I hate the hand holding!

I hate the stupid prayers!

Meetings don't help!

I hate speaking to other people!

I'm already sober. I don't need to go to meetings!

Every day a battle raged in my mind, a heated debate about why I *needed* to go versus why I didn't *want* to go.

Somehow, I managed to go almost every day for the first 90 days of my recovery (90 meetings in 90 days is encouraged for newcomers), and on nearly every one of those 90 days, I had to fight the urge to stay home instead.

One day I asked Paul the question that most people in recovery ask at some point.

"How long do I have to keep going to meetings?"

"Until you want to go," was the simple reply.

Huh?

At first, I didn't understand the answer. Until I *want* to go? Why would anyone WANT to go to a meeting? I go because I *have* to go, not because I *want* to go. I go because it keeps me from drinking (for some reason). That's it. Otherwise, meetings suck, and I'd rather stand on the street corner naked, chewing glass, than go to another damn meeting, thank you very much!

The idea that I might someday *want* to go to a meeting had never occurred to me. Paul's answer, of course, would eventually be proven correct.

It happened at my regular Thursday night meeting. The meeting was in a large hall, with about 75 people in attendance. This particular meeting always had a huge spread of amazing food brought by a group of women who were known as "old-timers," not because of their actual age, but because they had managed to stay sober for so many years. I'm convinced that one of the reasons the meeting was so popular was because of the food.

I arrived a few minutes early (which was happening

POLLUTED

more frequently) and loaded up a plate of food. I found a seat near the middle of the room (not in the back, another thing that was changing) and sat down to eat while I waited for the meeting to start. I didn't spot anyone I knew very well, but I nodded and smiled at a few people I recognized.

I sat there nibbling, watching a room filled with dozens of fellow drunks all talking loudly, laughing, and eating. The secretary was sitting at the front of the room. People were milling about, heading for their seats. There was a joyful tension in the air, the pre-show feeling that seems to proceed so many AA meetings that I've attended over the years.

As I munched on my grub (seriously, the food at this meeting was amazing!), it suddenly dawned on me that I was happy. Well, maybe not *happy*. I was content. That's a more accurate way to describe how I felt at that moment -- content.

I looked around, taking it all in. I sat in my seat, smiling to myself, realizing that I felt content and that I was glad to be there. I *wanted* to be there.

It was one of the best moments of my life. That's not an exaggeration. For the first time in years, I was content to be exactly where I was. I wasn't eager to leave. I didn't want to escape or get loaded. I felt no sense of panic or social anxiety. I felt peaceful and calm.

I knew what Paul had been talking about earlier. I wanted to be right there, where I was. I wanted to be at the meeting.

The Sound of My Voice

Being asked to speak at a meeting, or "lead" a meeting, is considered an honor and privilege in AA. The speaker shares his or her story with the room, setting the tone for the rest of the meeting. It's an opportunity to express what we have gone through, how we got there, and how sobriety is improving (or not improving) our life. In a nutshell, we discuss *what it was like* (drinking), *what happened* (why we stopped), and *what it's like now* (being sober).

For many people, being asked to lead a meeting is the most dreaded part of getting sober in AA, avoided at all costs. When it finally happens, it's like being invited to the electric chair; *take a seat so we can fry you like bacon.*

As a kid going through school, I hated two words with a passion that bordered on psychosis: ORAL REPORT. Oh, how I despised those words!

By now, I've made it abundantly clear that I've always struggled with shyness. The idea of speaking in front of a full classroom was the fear of all fears. Hearing my voice filling the void between the other kids and me was too much to take. By the time I got to college, I simply refused to do it, and would gladly accept the "F" rather than subject myself to the misery of public speaking.

Several months into my sobriety, the secretary of one of my morning meetings asked me to speak the following week. I tried to worm my way out of it with a stammering list of excuses, but he wouldn't take no for an answer (the bastard), so I reluctantly agreed.

For the next seven days, I was in complete panic mode. I couldn't sleep, concentrate, or eat. I was miserable. I shared my terror with Paul, who insisted I was going to survive. His advice was to just to tell my story in simple terms and to be honest. The essential part about speaking at a meeting is to be brutally honest. As long as I was honest, I couldn't go wrong.

That didn't help.

He also told me NOT to write down what I wanted to say. Instead, I should tell my story slowly and clearly as I remembered it, that the truth would carry the message.

Nope. Instead, I wrote down everything I could think of to say that would make me sound funny or cool. I tried to add a few jokes into the mix (always a bad idea), so everyone would be blown away by my brilliant sense of humor. I had this idea that if I could just dazzle everyone with my wit and genius than they would remain blind to the fact that I was a frightened man-child who had made some terrible mistakes in life and needed help to survive. If I could keep them laughing, they wouldn't realize that I was a pathetic loser who had nothing of any worth to offer the world.

When the day finally arrived, I thought I was going to

throw up the second I awoke. I was trembling with fear and apprehension. How can I get out of this? Maybe I can jam a knife into my eye so I can to go to the hospital instead? I once had a gun pointed at the side of my head during a mugging. Speaking at a meeting felt more frightening.

I decided to walk to the meeting instead of driving, hoping it would calm my nerves. It didn't. When I arrived, the room was buzzing with a few dozen people. My heart was pounding out of my chest as I took my seat next to the secretary (the bastard!).

The secretary started the meeting while I sat there freaking out, staring at the door, contemplating making a run for it.

Before I knew what was happening, the secretary introduced me. *God, I don't want to be here! Help!*

Somehow I managed to open my mouth and begin speaking. The sound of my voice filling that room was bizarre and unnerving. I spoke in a quivering tone, sweat streaming down my back. I kept my eyes on the floor to avoid looking at anyone. I stuck with the script I had written. I even told the stupid jokes, which got a few polite chuckles, but not much more.

I can honestly say I have no idea how I sounded or if I made any sense. When I finally finished (I spoke for about 20 minutes), the room erupted with applause. It felt amazing!

POLLUTED

It was normal to applaud a speaker when they finished. But this time, at this moment, they were clapping for *me*. They were letting me know that what I shared with them somehow mattered, that my story mattered, my words meant something. None of them cared if I was witty or cool. The only thing that mattered was that I found the courage to tell my story as best I could.

Paul and a few guys took me out for a celebratory breakfast after the meeting. They all knew what it was like to speak for the first time, and they let me know how proud of me they were.

For the rest of the day, I was on cloud nine, knowing that I had accomplished something meaningful. That day it felt that a dramatic event had occurred. I had crossed a line to a new life, one where I was able to express myself, to speak out, to share my story without shame, regret, or remorse. I had spoken in public, and I didn't die.

For the first time that I could remember, I felt proud of myself, like I had taken a huge leap forward in my recovery and my life.

Obsession

Even though I hadn't picked up a drink in several months, I still obsessed about drinking every day. I never stopped thinking about alcohol during waking hours. I dreamed about alcohol almost every night. If I spotted a liquor bottle in the store, my eyes would fixate on it like a moth contemplating a flame, my mouth watering. Going to a restaurant could be torturous if someone at a nearby table had a glass of wine or martini in front of them. I would stare at the glass with envy, fantasizing about the taste and sensation it created every time the person lifted it to their lips and swallowed, like watching booze porn.

I clearly remember going to a nice Italian restaurant with a sober friend. At the table next to us was a woman drinking a large glass of chardonnay. I couldn't take my eyes off it. The side of the glass glistened with condensation. Every ten minutes, she would lift the glass and take a teeny tiny sip, barely wetting her lips, before gently returning it to the table.

As I watched her, I became increasingly agitated and annoyed. Not because she was drinking wine, but because she was drinking it so *SLOWLY*! It started to infuriate me, those teeny tiny sips! Just take a *full fucking swallow*, would you? Pound it! By the time we finished our meal, she still hadn't finished her glass of wine. Half the wine was still in the glass! HALF! By the time we left, she STILL hadn't finished the drink.

I simply couldn't understand anyone drinking so slowly. If it were me, I would've finished a martini and a glass of wine before the waiter even took our order. The idea of making a single drink last an entire meal was utterly alien to me. It took me a long time to learn that not everyone inhales alcohol like oxygen. Normal people ("normies") can enjoy a glass of wine over an entire dinner, savoring the taste without the intention of pounding multiple drinks to get blind drunk. This concept was so far away from my mindset that it left me angry and bewildered to witness a normal adult enjoying a drink.

I had booze on my mind morning, noon, and night. The temptation to pick up a drink haunted me every hour of the day. Hell, every second of the day is more accurate. It seemed like I couldn't get away from it, either. Everywhere I turned, there it was.

We're surrounded by alcohol. Wherever you look, it's in your face. Alcohol is fetishized and sexualized in advertising to ensure you hand over your hard-earned money in exchange for the promise of excitement, wealth, and companionship. Companionship, in particular, is used in booze-marketing to capture our attention. The not-so-subtle message is if you just drink the right brand of alcohol, then you'll meet that hot, young mate that will make all of our problems disappear. Just buy the correct vodka, cognac, or wine, and the good life is waiting for you!

Someday I want to see an advertisement that shows

the car crash after the party, or the projectile vomiting the next morning, or the broken family crying at home. "*Drink our cognac and watch your life fall to pieces.*" Now that's an ad I'd love to see.

Going to AA meetings and talking with other alcoholics helped me get through each day without falling prey to my obsessive desires. I somehow managed to string together several months without drinking and was incredibly pleased with my accomplishment.

But I couldn't stop thinking about alcohol, no matter what! It was like going through a long, painful divorce; even though I knew the marriage had to end, I still had deep feelings for a wife who wanted to kill me. Not figuratively, but literally, kill me.

Then one day, it was just gone. There were no fireworks, no epiphany or sudden parting of the clouds. One day I woke up, and the obsession to drink, for whatever reason, was gone.

Poof! Like magic, it had vanished into the ether.

It was a strange sensation. I no longer felt an overwhelming desire to drink every moment of the day. The sight of a vodka bottle or six-pack of beer didn't cause my heart to pound in my chest. I had completely lost my desire to drink or get drunk. I was neither bothered by nor interested in alcohol.

There's not one particular event or revelation that I can identify which brought me to this moment. Perhaps it was just the accumulation of experiences over the last few months that had washed it away. Perhaps my body was finally getting used to life without alcohol. Maybe I was finally learning how to be comfortable in my skin. Maybe God played a hand in it. I have no idea, nor does it matter. I finally felt free from the obsession to drink, and that's all I cared about at that point.

There was still going to be many trials and challenges on the road ahead, many of them painful and difficult. But the day I had been hoping and praying for finally arrived, I was liberated. My obsession with alcohol had disappeared. A considerable part of my old life was gone, and my new life was just beginning.

STAGE 5 – HOPE

A New View

"Hope is the thing with feathers

That perches in the soul

And sings the tune without words

And never stops – at all."

-Emily Dickinson

Turning It Over

To move forward, I have to discuss a topic that many people want to gloss over or entirely bypass. But it's an inevitable part of sobriety (long-lasting sobriety, anyway), and I want to tackle it here by getting right to the point.

Sooner or later, every alcoholic who wants to stay sober has to ask the question: *Do I believe there is a power in the universe that is greater than me that can help me repair my life?*

The notion of a higher power frightens off a lot of people. It's astonishing how many people I've met over the years that simply refuse to consider the existence of any kind of higher power working in their life. They prefer, instead, to rely on themselves to provide all the answers and solutions to their problems. The tragic irony is that it was *their answers* and *solutions* that caused so much trouble in the first place. Most of the people I've met who refute the idea of a higher power entirely don't stay sober very long. Sad but true.

If alcoholics have one fatal flaw in common, it's our over-bloated sense of self. Our ego is our worst enemy. We think we have all the answers until one day we realize that our lives have turned into a cesspool, and we're drowning in our own shit (how's that for a subtle metaphor?).

I allowed my ego to lead me around for decades, and what I got in return was a life filled with addiction, remorse, debt, and sickness. It wasn't until I was willing to turn my life over to a power greater than myself that I was finally able to exorcise the demons that had haunted me for so long.

I'm going to skip over all the niceties and state clearly that I have faith in God. If you're a skeptic or atheist, that's fine. But for me, the only way I was able to get sober, and most importantly, STAY SOBER, is by placing my faith in a higher power that is active in my life. I'm not talking about religion. That's a discussion for another book. I'm talking about God. I don't claim to know what God is or even how God works in my life. But I know with absolute certainty that the moment I asked God for help, everything in my life changed for the better.

Not everyone comes to this decision easily. For many people, accepting the idea of a higher power is extremely difficult. It can take years to develop a comfortable understanding of what a higher power is and how it can be a source of strength in sobriety.

In AA, there's a lot of emphasis on turning our will and our lives over to God *as we understand God*. There's no definition offered regarding what God is or how we're supposed to find God. Instead, it's left up to each person to figure it out on their own, in their own time, based on their spiritual exploration. There are no lectures or lessons on God, nor expectations to follow or specific rules to learn. It's left entirely up to each of us to find God *as we understand God*.

POLLUTED

This is one of the great things about AA that I've always admired, providing a safe opportunity to choose what God is, and what God means to each of us, through personal investigation. Once the decision is left up to us individually, free from dogma or religion, we're free to explore the question any way we deem appropriate.

Early in my sobriety, I wasn't sure what to believe or where to look for answers to the endless questions I had regarding a higher power. So I listened to what others had to say about it, especially the old-timers who had been sober for years. What I slowly started to learn was that it didn't matter how I defined God (I find it best not to try), but to simply have faith that there is a force, or energy, of love working in my life that wants me to experience joy and peace.

The fact is -- and I state this based on years of experience -- that if I'm left on my own without faith in a higher power, I'm hopeless. I will quickly resort back to my self-destructive nature and probably repeat all the bad mistakes I made in the past, maybe even worse than before. But with faith in God, I live in an almost constant state of hope and optimism. Even on my bad days (and there are many), I always take comfort knowing that someone, or something, is watching over me, giving me the strength and hope I need to stay sober.

It's a tricky topic, the idea of God. It's difficult to place our trust in a power we can't see or touch. It requires desperation, courage, curiosity, and of course, faith. But for alcoholics like me, it's essential if I want to keep my sobriety and avoid the pain and suffering that brought me to my knees crying out for help.

Letting Go

I never realized how much I obsessed over the past until I was able to review it on paper. When I began working on Step Four with Paul, he had asked me to write down every single time I had been hurt in any way so that I could begin to forgive those who had harmed me. Step Eight, on the other hand, was my opportunity to write down every person I had ever screwed over so that I could prepare myself to apologize and make amends to all of them.

It was a long list.

It's a daunting task to remember and record every person you've ever hurt, deceived, ripped off, or betrayed. To see it all on paper is to confront the worst aspects of your personality. You quickly realize that you're not the blameless angel you imagined you were. There is nothing quite so humbling than to realize you've been a real asshole sometimes and hurt many people along the way.

As painful as the process can be, it's also a rare opportunity to cleanse away the guilt and shame that often poisons your psyche. Guilt is a very destructive emotion, and when left untreated, it will eat away at your soul. Making a list of all the people you have harmed intending to make amends to them is something I think everyone should try at least once in their life, alcoholic or not.

I spent several weeks working on my list, writing

down every detail I could remember about the people I had hurt. There were, of course, girlfriends I had betrayed or disrespected, as well as employers I had cheated. I even wrote down the kid I had beaten up in sixth grade. Our little schoolyard brawl had occurred over three decades ago, but I still felt a tremendous sense of shame every time I thought about punching him repeatedly while all the other kids hollered encouragement. My list also contained the many mistakes I had made as a direct result of my drinking.

Once I had it all down on paper, I was able to review it like a map that had led me to this point in my life. I could see all the hurt I had created in the world, the people I had punished, discarded, or crushed, simply because they didn't serve the purpose I expected or wanted from them.

It sounds horrible, I know, the idea of seeing how shitty we've been to certain people over the years. But it's more liberating than it sounds. This was my one chance to make things right. This was my opportunity to repair the wreckage I had left in my wake. This was my opportunity to correct the pain I had created.

Take a deep breath. Pray for guidance. The time to make things right had arrived.

Amends

To create an uncontaminated future, I had to clean up my polluted past. I tried to put off my amends (the "apology tour," as I like to call it) as long as possible. This is by far one of the most challenging things to face in recovery, reaching back into the past and asking forgiveness from a bunch of people, some of whom I hadn't seen or spoken with in 30 years.

Anyone who has ever faced this daunting task will agree that it's a lot like preparing for a root canal, knowing you won't receive novocaine. It's no accident that this is one of the last steps in the recovery process; otherwise, we wouldn't be psychologically or spiritually prepared to meet the challenge.

Paul gently encouraged me to move forward, starting with the easiest amends on my list and dealing with the big monsters later after I had some practice.

Finally, after much hesitation and agony, I began the arduous and often embarrassing task of tracking down the people I had harmed, first to make my apology, followed by the question: *is there anything I can do to make things right?*

Starting with the small amends was a wise suggestion. I was able to track down several old friends and girlfriends who I had deceived or hurt and made my apologies as best I could with a trembling voice and racing heart. Not a single person screamed at me, punched me, spit in my face, or rejected my apology. A few of them turned red with anger at being forced to remember a painful moment in their life. But that was as bad as it got, thank God.

Whew! I got through those without dying. Now it was time to face the real monsters in the closet, the ones when I had done serious harm.

The biggest one on my list was Mr. McCallister, my old music teacher from junior high school. Yes, junior high school! First, let me explain what I did to this poor guy.

As I stated in the opening, I began drinking when I was 12. By the time I was 13, I was also smoking weed, snorting coke, dropping acid, and eating mushrooms whenever they were available. I ran around with a group of long-haired kids, always doing our best to flaunt authority and act like tough guys. In reality, we were just a bunch of knuckleheads with bad attitudes and bad haircuts.

In our school, everyone had to take music appreciation class in 8th grade, which was taught by Mr. McCallister. We all loved him as a teacher. He was a bit of a hippy, laid back, part of the counter-culture of that time. There were rumors he liked to smoke pot, which made him instantly cool in our eyes. Most importantly, he was kind and patient with all the school losers, which meant my knucklehead friends and me. While all the popular kids sucked up to the math and science teachers, and the jocks sucked up to the PE teachers, we

POLLUTED

sucked up to the music teacher. I liked him so much that I even asked to be a teacher's assistant in his class. I couldn't believe my good fortune when my request was granted.

His classroom was like a dream for anyone who loved music (which I did). It was where the school chorus practiced every day and where all the instruments were stored. He also had an enormous collection of albums, including many rare records from the Beatles. He worked on weekends at a used-record store, so his personal collection, which he stored in the music class, was extensive and valuable. It was a fantastic place to spend time, and I loved being a part of that world, even for just an hour each day.

One Saturday afternoon, my friend Jeff and I were lingering around the school looking for trouble. We often spent time wandering the outdoor hallways at night and on weekends, which is odd since we professed to hate the place so much. We were both high on mushrooms, which we had washed down with a six-pack of beer.

One of us, I'm not sure who, got the brilliant idea to start lighting lockers on fire by dropping lit matches into the air vents on the front of each locker (again, knuckleheads). We ignited several lockers then ran laughing across the street and up to the top of a small hill near the school.

When we reached the top of the hill, the fire had climbed out of the lockers to engulf the building. It just so happened that the building was the music department.

Panicked and terrified, we ran for our lives as black smoke filled the sky. The next day, it was all over the local news. The entire building had burned to the ground. Instruments, Beatle's albums...everything had gone up in flames.

I carried that with me for thirty years -- thirty years of deep guilt and shame.

When I told Paul about this incident, he looked at me over the top of his glasses: "You know you have to track him down and make amends."

I was desperately hoping he'd say that since so many years had passed, I could simply let this one go. No such luck! Three decades had passed, and now I had to find the guy and apologize. Shit!

The crazy thing is that I found him in about 10 minutes. I called my old school and asked if there was a record of his whereabouts. It turns out he was still alive (secretly, I had hoped he was dead, so I wouldn't have to go through this) and teaching at a nearby college. After a few more calls, I finally managed to get his direct number at the campus.

I must've stared at my cell phone for an hour before I was able to build up enough courage to dial. I was nervous as hell, afraid of what he would say to me. In my head, he was going to curse me straight to hell, then hunt me down and stick a pitchfork in my ass before the devil had first shot.

POLLUTED

After just a few rings, he answered. "Mr. McCallister speaking."

I couldn't believe it was him on the other end of the line. After all those years had passed, I still recognized his voice.

I stumbled to find the right words.

"Mr. McCallister, my name is Dirk Foster. You probably don't remember me, but I was one of your students about thirty years ago."

He very politely said, "Your name sounds familiar. How are you?"

"Well, I'm not sure. I have something I need to speak with you about..." I was starting to tremble.

"Okay. Go ahead."

"It's about the fire, the one that burned down your classroom."

Dead silence.

I felt panic rising in my chest. I wanted to hang up the phone.

"Um," I continued, "that was me. I'm the one who started it. It was an accident. I never meant to do it. It just..., I'm so sorry. I'm the one who burned down your class."

I didn't bother to mention Jeff, my co-conspirator. No reason to drag him into this insane situation. I was cleaning up my past, not Jeff's.

There was a long, heavy silence. So I just continued babbling.

"Here's the thing, I'm a recovering alcoholic. To stay sober, I have to clean up the wreckage of my past. That means I have to make amends to all the people I have harmed in my life. And what I did...burning down your classroom was one of the worst things I ever did. It was an accident...I don't know what to say. I'm so sorry. I'm so sorry. I know you probably can't forgive me, but I want you to know how sorry I am, and I will do anything in my power to make it right."

I could hear him breathing. The silence continued.

Finally, he cleared his throat and started to speak softly.

"To be honest, I've wondered my entire life what happened that day. I thought maybe someone did it on purpose. A lot of the kids thought I was odd. I figured someone had it in for me. I always just assumed it was intentionally set. I lost a lot that day, things that were valuable to me. Things I cherished."

Tears began to pool in my eyes. The idea that he had carried this with him all these years was devastating.

"It wasn't on purpose," I said quietly. "I promise. We were high, just being idiots. We loved you; all of us did. It was an accident."

"I believe you," he said. "I also want you to know that my brother is a recovering alcoholic, too. So I know about the amends."

And this is where it got really crazy.

He continued: "I accept your apology, Dirk. And I want to thank you sincerely for calling me and letting me know. This must be a tough call for you to make, and I admire your courage. This brings me a lot of relief. It's bothered me for so long. I can finally let it go now that I know the truth."

"Is there anything I can do to make it right with you," I asked.

"Yes," he replied. "Just stay sober. If you promise to do your best to stay sober than we're good. That's all I ask. Just stay sober."

By this point, I was starting to lose control of my emotions. I promised over and over again that I would do everything in my power to stay sober.

"Thanks for calling, Dirk. And good luck."

When I hung up the phone, I felt blessed. As the tears rolled down my cheeks, I understood for the first time what it means to receive grace.

Forgiveness

Forgiveness from others is a blessing. Forgiving ourselves is a necessity.

By the time I completed my amends list, I was exhausted. More importantly, I felt an enormous sense of relief. I had faced up to the pain I had caused others and made things right to the best of my abilities. I certainly didn't do it perfectly, no one ever does. But I did my best to meet the challenge and asked for, and mostly received, forgiveness from those I had hurt.

Forgiving myself, however, would prove to be more difficult. I still carried a lot of shame for the way I had conducted my life, especially in the last few years of my drinking. I found it incredibly painful to realize how much time I had wasted pursuing oblivion from a bottle. How could I have allowed this to happen? Why didn't I jump off the train of addiction earlier? Why had I polluted my body, mind, and spirit to such an extent that it almost killed me?

There is an ongoing debate about the cause of alcoholism, whether it's a disease we're born with or something we learn from our environment. Is it nature or nurture? Do we learn to become alcoholics through our environment (nurture), or are we born with a specific propensity to be alcoholics (nature)?

I think it's a combination of both.

I believe that I have a genetic predisposition to addiction, which runs in my family. Not only do I drink alcoholically, but I also do other things "alcoholically." Whether its cigarettes, sugar, or television, I often overindulge to the point of excess. When I find something that takes away stress, boredom, fear or pain, I pursue it with abandon. I have a deep need for escapism in any form.

However, I'm also convinced that I've learned many of my self-destructive habits from sources outside of myself. I grew up in a time when alcohol and drug use (and abuse) were considered fun and cool. And if there was anything I wanted when I was young, it was to be considered fun and cool. Our culture is awash in mind-altering substances that promise a means of temporary escape, glorified through smart marketing and social conformity. Like millions of other people, I have fallen victim to advertising and peer pressure that told me drinking was not only acceptable but would help me cope with life while having a great time. Not only would my life be more exciting if I drank and used, but I'd also be sexier ad more impressive because of it. Hell, yes! Sign me up! Open the bottle and pour that shit down my throat!

- Was I born with a disease called alcoholism? *Yes.*

- Did I learn a lot of bad habits from the world around me? *Absolutely.*

- Could I have sought help earlier, before it took control of my life? *Without doubt.*

- Am I to blame for being an alcoholic? *It doesn't matter. I AM an alcoholic, and the sooner I face the facts and deal with it, the sooner I'll find peace.*

Once I was able to start reconciling these truths in my mind, the process of forgiving myself became easier. Like all difficult challenges, it took time before I was entirely able to forgive myself for the life I had lived in addiction. Even to this day, I occasionally feel regret for the years I lost to alcoholism. Yet there's nothing I can do about it other than take comfort knowing that I was born with a disease that will never be cured, only managed. And many of the bad habits I picked up along the way were absorbed by forces that permeate society.

One morning, after I had finished my amends, I stood before the mirror in my apartment bathroom, preparing to shave. This was the same mirror in which I had spit at my reflection when I was still drinking, disgusted by the site of my face.

On this morning, I felt good, blessed to be sober and forgiven by others. I managed to smile into the mirror and said out loud, without embarrassment:

"I forgive you."

Shifting

Once I was able to begin forgiving myself, my view of the world started to change, too. In a way, the new sense of optimism I experienced was similar to the pink cloud stage I had passed through earlier in my recovery. There were moments, sometimes entire days, when I felt an intense excitement about being alive. The difference was that I finally had substantial evidence of positive things I had accomplished. I was now able to feel proud of the progress I was making in recovery:

- I hadn't touched a drop of alcohol in several months
- I was getting healthier by not drinking
- I had accepted that I was sick and needed help
- I was doing what my sponsor told me (mostly)
- I was sleeping better most nights
- I was taking better care of my body
- I was letting go of deeply held resentments
- I was developing my faith in God
- I was making new sober friends
- I was going to meetings every day
- I was learning how to speak out loud
- I had made amends to the people I had hurt
- I had forgiven myself

Finally, I had a growing track record that I could point to that helped me stay out of the depression that always followed the pink cloud euphoria.

I was beginning to shift in a new direction. My outlook on life was becoming stronger and more hopeful. The overwhelming desire to ESCAPE life was slowly being replaced by an urge to feel and experience life. Instead of running from how I felt, I was beginning to experience "*life on life's terms*" and enjoying the ride.

For most of my life, I had attempted to control my moods and emotions through alcohol. When I felt sad, I drank. When I felt depressed, I drank. When I felt afraid, I drank. When I felt happy, I drank. No matter what I was going through emotionally, I would drink to either suppress negative feelings or enhance positive ones. Either way, I was always altering my mood by drinking to change or improve how I felt.

Normal people ("normies") often assume that alcoholics only drink so they don't feel bad or depressed. But in my experience, we also drink to enhance the good feelings. It's not enough to just feel happy or positive. Why not take it to the next level? If I'm feeling good *without* alcohol, just think how great I'll feel *with* alcohol. I don't want to feel good, that's not enough. I want to feel AMAZING! Some of my worst, most destructive nights of drinking resulted from my desire to improve good feelings.

Learning how to "live life on life's terms" was one of the

many gifts I received in recovery. Accepting that sometimes I was going to feel bad, and sometimes I was going to feel good, and being perfectly fine with either, was life-changing.

I certainly wasn't perfect at it, by any means. There was still going to be many situations in the coming months and years when I would get so depressed or anxious that the only thing I could do was to reach for a tub of ice cream or a bag of jelly doughnuts to "fix" how I was feeling. But relying on sweets to alter my mood was far better than turning to whiskey and cocaine, so I learned to accept that sometimes I just needed something sweet and outside of myself to make me feel better.

My attitude was changing. I was feeling hopeful about each day and accepting that some days just suck. I was learning to live life on life's terms, good or bad, for better or worse.

Awakening

I've always liked the word "somnambulist," which is a fancy way of saying "sleepwalker." I prefer the fancy version (perhaps *pretentious* is more accurate), because I think it makes me sound smart when I use it in a sentence.

As I continued to make peace with my past, I realized that I had been walking through my life half asleep, *like a somnambulist searching for a way to escape a dark and chaotic dream* (See how I did that? Yes it's pretentious, but it sounds so cool!).

Much of my life had involved running from fear and discomfort, always reaching for a way to "fix" the problem with a steady stream of liquid relief. Now, I was learning that I didn't necessarily have to fix myself all the time. Instead, I could just accept whatever emotion I was experiencing and work through it instead of working against it. Rather than always trying to suppress or run from feelings, I was learning to embrace whatever I felt, good or bad.

I was learning how to live in the present moment, not the past or future, grateful for every experience.

I was allowing myself to feel everything. I no longer had the constant need to control every aspect of my existence. Life, in many ways, is like the weather. Hot or cold, sunlight or snowfall, the weather is completely out of my hands, something I can't control. My only choice is to enjoy the day, rain, or shine. All I can do is wake up in the morning and do the best I can with what's in front of me, hour by hour. Realizing this, I became more relaxed and more open to learning new things.

Finally I was free from the resentment, shame, and guilt I had carried for so long. I was ready to move into the next stage of my recovery. It's incredible how much relief we can find when we're able to let go of the past, cherish the present, and not worry about the future. I was waking up from a long, arduous dream, a somnambulist finally emerging from his dark and dreary slumber (See how I did that?).

STAGE 6 – JOY

Learning to Crawl

"It is never too late to be what you might have been."

-George Eliot

Learning to Crawl

I was quickly approaching twelve months of sobriety, and my life had changed dramatically. I still struggled with insecurity and shyness, but I no longer allowed it to hold me back from doing the things I had wanted to do. When I felt fear rising, I was learning just to say "fuck it," and keep moving forward despite my apprehension. I was hungry for life, eager to recapture much of what I had lost over the decades, especially the last ten years of my drinking.

I refer to my thirties as "my lost decade." Large chunks of those years I can't remember or prefer to forget. While most people my age were starting to raise children and build careers, I had spent my thirties in a daze, desperately trying to drown sorrow and resentment in a river of booze. The subsequent lifestyle that accompanied the lost decade had left me empty, sick, and broken.

Now it was time to recapture what I had forsaken, or at the very least, give it my best effort.

Effort is an essential part of any meaningful endeavor. Ultimately, the results of any action are out of my hands. Leave the results, as they say, to God. The only thing that I can control in my life is the effort I put into every situation. The effort, not the conclusion, is the fun part of the game. The effort is where we find joy.

I kept my efforts simple at first. Clean my apartment

every day. Make my bed. Shower and shave each morning. Eat healthier food. Take a twenty minute walk. Go to a meeting. Be kind to people, even when I don't want to be kind. It's incredible how much self-respect and satisfaction can be derived from the simplest actions.

I began to branch out into areas of life that I wanted to explore or improve, including my hunger to learn. I was starving for spiritual awareness and started reading everything I could get my hands on about recovery, addiction, religion, and self-improvement. I would browse libraries and bookstores for hours. Books became a refuge that helped me focus my mind and expand my knowledge.

There were so many things I wanted to know and experience. I was like a baby learning to crawl, looking at the world with intense curiosity, eager to explore one thing after another, unperturbed by self-doubt or apprehension. The way I figured it, I had survived more than my share of danger and hazards. I wasn't going to let anything stop me from growing, regardless of any fear or doubt I encountered along the way.

I had given up too much of my youth. Now was the time to get some of it back and reclaim the years lost to addiction.

Rusty Jalopy

When I first got sober, I was in terrible physical shape. I was pale, pudgy, and soft as a marshmallow. I could barely walk up a flight of stairs without panting. I suffered from horrible stomach pains morning, noon, and night. I experienced frequent migraines. I couldn't sleep. My diet consisted mostly of cheeseburgers, ramen noodles, soda, and milkshakes. I considered cigarettes to be a major food group.

The idea of exercising and eating healthy was the farthest thing from my mind when I was drinking. You could just as easily have asked me to saw off my thumb with a butter knife. Exercise at that stage consisted of walking to the liquor store for the third bottle of wine or running up the stairs to my drug dealer's apartment. That was as far as my workout routine ever went.

With my newfound hope and optimism, I made a conscious decision that I was going to get physically fit.

But how would I begin this miraculous transformation? There was still a lot of damage to repair. I felt like a decrepit, old car that had been sitting in the backyard for decades, abandoned and overrun by rust and decay. Rebuilding and repairing the Jalopy called my body was going to be a daunting task.

Like all epic journeys, I had to start with a single step,

literally. I began to walk every day, sometimes several times per day. I would walk to the grocery store. I would walk to AA meetings. I would walk to the book store. I would walk to the coffee shop. I would walk without a destination. Walking became my first form of exercise in those early days. It was also a great form of meditation, though I wasn't aware of that right away.

I became a walking fanatic, and I loved it. Best of all, I started to slowly lose weight because of all the miles I was covering.

After a few weeks, I did the unthinkable. I began to JOG. I'll be honest; jogging is probably my least favorite thing in the world. In fact, I hate it. But I knew it would speed up my effort to get in shape, so when I went for my daily walks, I would incorporate a short jog into the routine. Walk five blocks, jog one block. Walk five blocks, jog one block. Eventually, I was able to jog five blocks and walk one block, which had a significant impact on my physical condition.

Soon, I transferred my walking/jogging routine to short hikes around the hills near my home. Hiking became a passion, something I wanted to do as often as possible. I loved being outdoors in nature, something I cherish to this day, and the physical exertion, especially on my lungs and heart, helped to accelerate my weight loss even faster.

I was well aware that getting fit was going to be a slow process. But I stuck with it, eventually joining a local gym.

POLLUTED

I began to work out with weights and, more importantly, started to practice yoga. Yoga was one of the best things I did for myself in early recovery. It had a significant impact on my overall health and state of mind. If there is any single form of exercise I would recommend to someone who is getting sober, yoga would be at the top of the list.

I was finally beginning to take care of myself. I was putting a concerted effort into repairing the physical damage inflicted on my body from years of neglect and substance abuse. I was feeling better, sleeping well most night, and my confidence started to rise.

The decrepit, old Jalopy, was slowly coming back to life.

Full Pockets

To my great surprise and delight, I noticed early in my sobriety that I seemed to have more money. Once I stopped spending every extra nickel on booze, cigs, and blow, I suddenly had money to spend on things like food, gas, and rent.

This is one of the first things many people discover; as soon as they quit wasting all their funds getting loaded, magically, they have cash in their pockets when they wake up in the morning. Imagine waking up WITH cash and WITHOUT a hangover. Miracles do happen!

Having money in my pockets added a new dimension of joy to my recovery. I was able to buy things I wanted or needed without freaking out or scheming. Meeting my financial obligations became easier.

Granted, I was also in deep debt. I owed a lot of money on a car I couldn't afford and had ruined my credit over the years. This was a serious issue that I would have to fix. Part of recovery in AA includes repairing the financial damage we've done to our lives through irresponsible behavior. Many of us mess things up financially while we're drinking. I certainly did. I can't count how many times I hid from landlords, credit card companies, and banks, hoping they would leave me alone when payments were due each month.

If we drink long enough and hard enough, every detail

POLLUTED

of our lives becomes infected. The lifestyle that accompanies long term alcoholism seeps into every corner of our existence, poisoning things that normal people handle without difficulty or drama. Money is one aspect of life that many heavy drinkers struggle to manage. Not that there aren't plenty of wealthy alcoholics who never have a financial care in the world. However, the majority of people who spend years or decades drinking alcoholically do significant damage to their financial condition.

I was one of those people. I screwed things up royally, and it was going to take time to make things right. Eventually, slowly over a few years, I would fix all the financial damage I had done and repair my credit. It wasn't easy, but eventually, I got it done (if you're struggling with money issues, I wrote a book called "Sober and Broke" that might help).

In the short term, I always seemed to have money in my pocket, which was strange to get used to at first. I was so accustomed to being flat broke all the time that I was slightly confused by the sight of cash in my wallet each day.

Having money was certainly better than being broke. It improved how I was feeling and offered a great deal of relief and happiness to my recovery. I was starting to feel like an adult, which was pretty strange.

Serenity: An Inside Job

I had spent the better part of my life trying to drink away my problems. My goal was always to subdue the fear and anger that swirled inside my head. It wasn't until I was able to remove the numbing agent of alcohol from my body and mind that I realized I was searching for peace, both mentally and spiritually. Once the booze was removed from my life, I needed to replace it with something else that would fill the void and bring comfort and serenity to my chaotic brain.

Meditation proved to be the source of strength, hope, and serenity I was seeking.

Before I started meditating, I didn't understand what it was or how it works. The easiest way to describe meditation is to call it *mind-training*. If we can go to the gym to train our bodies, then we can go to our minds to train our thinking. Every time we practice meditation, we're trying to train our minds to be calm and quiet and to accept life as it is (i.e., *life on life's terms*).

When I first tried to meditate, the noise in my brain was loud and confusing. Every time I closed my eyes to meditate, I was bombarded by multiple thoughts and ideas, all crashing together, each one demanding my attention. There was a tornado of activity swirling inside my head. I was unable to hold a single thought for more than a few seconds before another idea, or disturbing image would blow through the

POLLUTED

door of my subconscious and twist and spin across my brain.

I would quickly open my eyes, startled by the chaos inside my mind. Some thoughts were amusing, while others were frightening. I would close my eyes and try again, only to quickly open them as soon as the thought-storm commenced. It was overwhelming.

Thankfully, I stuck with it and never gave up. Over several weeks and months, I slowly began to incorporate simple techniques that allowed me to sit for longer and longer periods with my eyes closed while I tried to focus on my breath. Being able to sit with my eyes shut for five minutes was a huge accomplishment. Eventually, I could sit for twenty to thirty minutes peacefully.

When I began meditation, I was searching for a way to find serenity. I knew I had a disturbed and restless ("untrained") mind. If there was a way for me to quiet the noise in my head and soothe my aching spirit, I was determined to find it.

Our mind is a lot like a garage filled with junk that has accumulated over many years. We know the garage needs to be cleaned, but we keep putting it off as long as possible. Then one day, we turn on the light and are confronted by a mountain of rubbish. Sooner or later, we have to empty the garage, or the problem is going to keep getting worse.

When I first confronted the rubbish heap in my brain, I was shocked by how much garbage I had been hoarding.

It's shocking and sad to look back on it now and realize the amount of negative crap I had accumulated over my lifetime. As I advanced in my meditation practice, I began to learn that most of my negative thoughts were a result of selfish craving. I craved wealth, power, popularity, sex, influence, and glory. I wanted the world to recognize my greatness and adore me. Since that wasn't how things had turned out, my cravings eventually turned into bitterness, which I tried to drown in booze.

One of the great things about meditation is that it allows us an opportunity to recognize our source of suffering in order to release it. If we're able to see what is causing us pain (negative thought), we can then identify it for what it is and let it go with a smile. We can train our minds to release the negative thoughts that hold us hostage. Empty our minds of destructive cravings, and our minds will fill with acceptance, peace, and joy.

I often use the image of a red helium balloon being released into the sky. Once I have identified a negative thought, instead of holding onto it, I think of it as a balloon that I want to float away. I let it go and watch as it drifts upwards into the clouds, finally disappearing out of sight. Perhaps it sounds too simplistic, but it often works.

There are times when negative thoughts are buried so deep and are so painful, that we need to seek professional help to dislodge them. But meditation can be helpful to

POLLUTED

almost anyone looking to explore the inner workings of their mind so that they can begin letting go of the harmful debris they've been hoarding.

Meditation was, and is, one of the essential factors in my recovery, helping me immensely by calming the storms that once raged inside my head and replacing it with the peace and serenity I had been searching for my entire life.

Back to Work

Early recovery is like a full-time job. It takes up most of your waking hours and requires dedication and hard work. There are many struggles along the journey that, hopefully, result in more successes than failures. Ultimately, the harder we work, the greater the rewards we reap.

Having spent the better part of a year completely immersed in my recovery, I was starting to feel more confident and optimistic than I had in my entire life. I say that without exaggeration. I felt good about myself and the path I was following. I was no longer imprisoned by my addiction nor poisoned by fear and resentment. I was learning how to cultivate hope and serenity. I was sleeping better, eating better, exercising, meditating, and attempting to repair my finances.

Not that I was entirely out of danger from relapse. I never will be. Protecting my sobriety is a lifelong endeavor, a job that never ends (*yikes*). This is just the reality I have learned to accept, like a diabetic who has to be forever proactive about taking insulin and eating correctly. I have to do whatever it takes, every day, to remain clean.

Whatever danger there was for me in the world, I was ready to face it head-on.

One of my biggest challenges has always been interacting with other people. In AA, I was surrounded by others like me, all of us helping each other fight the battle of recovery. But at some point I knew I had to get back out into the world of "normal people," meaning people who don't spend all their time focusing on drinking or not drinking (or as Shakespeare might say: *to drink or not to drink, that is the question*).

It took me a long time to realize that not everyone is obsessed with alcohol and drugs. Most people spend the majority of their time focusing on things like family, careers, vacations, and paying bills. While I had spent decades pickling myself in alcohol, other people were out creating real lives and fulfilling real dreams. I wanted to figure out how to join that world while still maintaining my presence on the island of broken toys called AA.

My reintroduction back into the world of normal people started when I took an assignment as a freelance publicist for a small company. For several years before getting sober, I worked as an independent public relations consultant. I worked with anyone who would hire me. I wasn't too picky about whom I worked for or how much I got paid as long as their checks didn't bounce. I had a background in corporate marketing (having lost every job due to my drinking), so I was able to piece together enough freelance work to feed my drinking habit and keep the lights turned on in my apartment.

The new job was pretty simple; I was to promote the company (a consumer electronics business) to the media and develop the company's online visibility through a steady stream of press releases and news stories.

The most significant part about this assignment was that it required I occupy an office within their corporate headquarters. This would mean showing up each morning (on time!) like an employee, as well as interacting daily with the regular staff. In other words, I had to show up every day and talk to other humans.

I was nervous but took the assignment without hesitation. Feel the fear and do it anyway.

The job was temporary and only lasted a few months, but it was a great experience. I showed up on time every morning, NOT hungover. I worked at my desk all day and achieved excellent results for the company. Most importantly, I felt comfortable interacting with the people in the building, who were all friendly and kind. And when I was required at times to speak in front of the management staff, I didn't panic and hardly blushed (though I did blush a little).

I did my job without bursting into flames. And I never had the urge to run out of the door and drink. Not once.

This was the first of many new clients I was to land. Equipped with the confidence and self-discipline that I had developed in sobriety, I was able to build my freelance business into a lucrative operation that sustained me for years to come and helped me climb out of debt.

POLLUTED

    I was finally starting to interact in the world, taking slow steps forward as I continued to rebuild my life. And when things got difficult or I became overwhelmed with anxiety, the people in AA were ready and willing to help. I was learning how to straddle both worlds-- the world of normal people and the world of broken toys -- and starting to feel comfortable in both.

Freedom

There had been so many changes over the last eleven months that it was difficult to keep track. In a relatively short period, everything had changed dramatically. I was clean and sober and improving every part of my life – mind, body, spirit, and even finances. I was staying busy, being productive with my time, making new friends in and out of AA, and getting healthier by the day.

One bright, clear morning, I was walking towards my favorite coffee shop. I had developed a ritual of waking up early, meditating for twenty minutes, then walking to the coffee shop where I'd read the paper and watch people (people-watching is one of my favorite hobbies). I loved this daily routine. I also loved the fact that I was rising at a decent hour each day, feeling rested, and without the bitter hangovers that had made mornings painful for so many years.

On this one particular morning, heading for my coffee, I began to look around at all the trees that lined the sidewalk. It was like I had never noticed them before. They looked beautiful, swaying gently in the wind as birds flitted amongst their branches. The air was fresh and crisp. The sky was bright blue, a few fluffy clouds drifting overhead.

I stopped in my tracks to stare at the world around me, taking it all in, appreciating my neighborhood for the first time.

POLLUTED

In that moment I experienced deep contentment and joy. It washed through me in warm waves. I was acutely aware that I had passed through the most difficult challenge of my life and had come out on the other side, free from the demons that had haunted me for so long, cleansed of resentment and anger, and hopeful for the future. For the first time, I felt happy, joyous, and free.

I stood there for about five minutes, allowing the warmth to run through me. Then I bowed my head, said a short prayer of thanks, and continued on my way.

STAGE 7 – PURPOSE

What Matters Most

"Believe in your heart that you're meant to live a life full of passion, purpose, magic and miracles"

-Roy T. Bennett

365

There are milestones in every person's life that stand high above the rest -- moments when we reach a goal that once seemed unattainable. Achieving one year of sobriety was the defining experience of my life. Early in my recovery, reaching five days without a drink seemed like a miracle. Now I had made it an entire year clean and sober, which seemed unreal. Somehow I had managed not to take a single sip of alcohol for three hundred and sixty-five days. When I woke up that morning, I was astonished to realize what I had achieved.

I eagerly rushed to my morning meeting, where I received my one-year sobriety chip. I stood before a room of thirty people and thanked everyone, especially the people who had the most significant impact on my recovery, Paul in particular. Instead of feeling stage-fright, I was proud to be standing there, eager to let my voice fill the room: no blushing or stammering, just words of gratitude flowing out of me.

Over the years since that day, I've watched many people take five-year chips, 10-year chips, 25-year chips, and even longer. Every one of them is a massive accomplishment that deserves respect and recognition. But nothing fills me with as much joy and excitement as seeing a person take a one year chip. I get emotional every time. That first year is always the most difficult one to achieve, the time when we are most vulnerable to relapse and defeat. Watching anyone take a one year chip is also a great reminder of where I once was, and where I never hope to return.

After one year, I certainly wasn't "cured" or safe from relapse; I never will be. I will always have to work consciously to protect my sobriety, no matter how long I remain clean. But on that day, I felt reborn into a new life filled with optimism and hope. I was ready to conquer the world. If I could stay sober that long, perhaps I could accomplish other goals. Maybe I could recapture some of the years I'd lost to drinking.

For every alcoholic who's managed to get sober, similar questions always arise: *What have I lost? What parts of my life can I regain? Is it too late to recapture my dreams? How do I start over?*

During that first year, I was completely immersed in the process of staying sober. My life was placed on hold in order to concentrate exclusively on learning how to live free from alcohol and other self-destructive habits. Now, one year sober, the time had arrived to get back to finding what it was I wanted from my life, and how to go about achieving my goals and dreams, even if I was getting a late start.

I was 44 years old, and my life was just beginning.

Others

One of the most crucial aspects of long-term recovery in AA is our obligation to help other alcoholics navigate the treacherous waters of sobriety.

When we first get sober, the only thing we can focus on is cleaning up the mess we've made of our own lives. But at some point, we need to turn our attention to others, passing along what we've learned so they too can benefit from our "experience, strength and hope." Helping others can take countless forms – driving them to a meeting, talking to them, answering their late-night calls, or keeping them company when they're lonely or frightened. We can also work with others by taking them through the 12 steps ("sponsoring") as Paul did with me.

Helping others in recovery is something I think everyone should do, whether they get sober through AA or not. Watching someone repair and rebuild their life after addiction is to witness a miracle. Best of all, it reminds us that we need to remain diligent about our recovery. By helping others, we have a better chance of avoiding relapse.

After I had received my hard-earned one year chip, I began to focus more on giving my time to other people in recovery. Paul was an excellent example for me to follow. He was always helping someone, continually giving his time and compassion to some poor bastard stumbling into his first meeting as I had a year earlier, broken and desperate for help. He made it very clear to me that if I wanted to keep my sobriety, I had to give it away and share what I had learned.

At first, I was reluctant. I was still the center of my universe and wasn't crazy about diverting my attention away from ME to help someone else. Selfishness, more than benevolence, was always my default mode. But over the last twelve months, I'd learned that the wisest thing for me to do was follow Paul's advice about most subjects, so I decided I would do what he suggested and see where I landed.

Where I landed was in a car with several sober friends, visiting hospitals and rehabs, discussing our experience as recovering alcoholics. We would volunteer our time each week to participate as a visiting "panel," which is just another way of saying we brought an AA meeting to these facilities. Most of the people we spoke to were in rough shape, many of them having survived recent overdoses. Others were fresh out of psych wards or prison.

These were strange and often hilarious adventures. There we were, a bunch of recovering drunks who could barely manage our own lives, talking to a bunch of drunks who could barely manage to put a sentence together. Half of them were drooling, nodding off, or still hallucinating. Our little group would be at the front of the room, telling our stories and trying to sound profound about the dangers of addiction, while most of our audience would be either asleep, nodding

POLLUTED

off, or staring at the ceiling.

At times it felt futile like these people were just too far gone to care about anything we had to say. But occasionally, someone would approach us after the meeting to ask questions about the 12 steps or how to live sober. Some of the people we spoke to genuinely wanted to get better. They knew they were sick and needed help, and something we had said sparked their desire to finally get clean. Those were the moments that made it all worthwhile. Helping others, I soon learned, could feel pretty damn good.

Over the years, I've sponsored several people and spoke on numerous panels and at countless AA meetings. I've even had the honor of helping multiple friends in their recovery, people I used to party with in my younger days.

One thing I've learned is that addiction is spread out in the world far and wide. It's everywhere, and no one is immune. I've worked with alcoholic professors, plumbers, lawyers, burglars, doctors, cooks, artists, ex-cons, and cops. One thing all of us have in common is an addiction that has the power to crush the strongest man or woman and leave their lives devastated and destroyed. Working with others is the best way to ensure long term success at fighting a disease that often takes the lives of even the mightiest among us.

God

I'm going to circle back to a topic I covered earlier because it's one of the most crucial parts of my recovery and helps direct every action I take in recovery.

I once heard a close friend refer to God as "Santa Claus in the sky." He was being facetious, of course, trying to make the point that believing in God is like believing there's a bearded man in the sky randomly handing out gifts (or not). Even though I had developed faith by then, I still thought it was funny. I had been agnostic most of my life, so I completely understood his point of view.

I've always been uncomfortable with organized religion. It often appears to be nothing more than a tool used to control people through guilt and fear. In college, I learned about Karl Marx and his statement that "religion is the opium of the masses," meaning it's supposed to anesthetize people to make them compliant and submissive. As far as I was concerned, religion was a business, and God was an abstraction.

Then my life fell to pieces, and I fell to my knees, pleading for help. On that day, God became much more than an abstraction. Once I began to pray and trust in a conscious force of love in the universe, every part of my life changed in a positive direction. I'm still uncomfortable with certain parts of organized religion, but relying on God is like breathing air; I can't live without it.

POLLUTED

Many people enter sobriety either without faith of any kind or with considerable doubt. I get it. For me, however, relying on God has become the cornerstone of my sobriety. I simply can't imagine how I would survive without faith in a Higher Power that responds to prayer and guides me. There have been countless times over the last 12 years when I was crippled by depression or fear when nothing helped until I prayed to a God of my understanding. It's worked every single time.

Faith in God gives my life much of its purpose because it continually challenges and inspires me. Investigating the presence of God has become one of my primary goals and passions. I will never find all the answers while I'm still alive, but the journey of faith and my trust in God feeds my curiosity and nourishes my soul.

Maybe God is like Santa Claus after all because faith, like sobriety, has been an endless gift.

Family

The closest I ever came to relapsing was during the last few months of my father's life as he died slowly and painfully from cancer.

Like many father-son relationships, ours was complicated at times. There were times in my life when I felt extremely close to my dad. Growing up, I never worshipped professional athletes or movie stars. My dad was the only hero I ever had. As a child, he could do no wrong in my eyes.

He was also a man with distinct flaws that made his relationship with his three sons often distant and awkward. There were times when we didn't see him for long periods, as if he lived on another planet. He was kind, ambitious, generous, and loved to laugh and tease. He could also be sarcastic and cruel, especially when he drank too much wine, which was often.

For whatever reason, he seemed to direct much of his sarcasm and razor-sharp tongue in my direction when we were growing up. Even as an adult, he could crush my self-esteem after a few glasses of cabernet. Dinner time with dad could either be a laugh riot or a lesson in the brutality of verbal jabs. As much as I adored him, I also felt inadequate and nervous whenever I was in his presence. Even when cancer had reduced him to nothing more than a shell of the man he once was, he still held a power over me that was astonishing.

POLLUTED

At the age of forty-eight, I often blushed and stuttered when I spoke with my father while standing over his death bed.

I was three years sober when he was diagnosed with bladder cancer. I was five years sober when he passed away. I believe with complete certainty that God led me to recovery so that I would be able to help him and my family during his last years; otherwise, I would've been useless to all of them.

In his final months, my brothers and I took turns watching our dad and stepmother, who was in the early stages of Alzheimer's. To say it was a difficult time doesn't come close to describing what we went through as my father lay dying while my stepmother couldn't remember his name. There were days when the sadness and pain seemed unbearable.

I spent much of this time in silent prayer, asking for guidance and strength. But the temptation to drink was often overwhelming. His apartment was stocked with wine. And there were enough prescription narcotics near his bed to supply a drug store. There were many nights, after he and my stepmother had fallen asleep, that I sat in that dark apartment fighting the intense urge to sneak a drink or maybe ten. And the morphine bottle next to his bed looked particularly appealing, even though I had never been interested in heroin or opioids.

Thankfully, I was able to attend AA meetings whenever I could get a break. When I couldn't get to a meeting, I would either sneak off to pray or call Paul or other friends from AA to talk me off the ledge. I managed to stay sober the entire time.

I told dad I loved him every day, sometimes several times per day, and kissed his forehead every night before he drifted off into restless sleep. I also administered morphine drops below his tongue when the pain became too much for him to handle anymore.

I was lying on a couch at the foot of his bed the night he died, sober and grateful that I could be of service to my father and the rest of my family when it mattered the most.

Home

I had been visiting Lake Tahoe since I was a child and considered it one of the most beautiful spots on earth. In the first few years of my sobriety, I began to take trips to the lake every chance I could. I'd been living in Los Angeles for more than two decades and was starting to feel that maybe it was time to replace pavement and smog with rivers and lakes.

When I'd first moved to Los Angeles, shortly after college, I was determined to become a brilliant and successful screenwriter. I had wanted to be a writer since the 5th grade, and screenwriting seemed easy and lucrative. I read a magazine article about how much writers were making in Hollywood, so I figured why not give that a try.

As I was to find out, writing screenplays is a lot easier than selling them.

I spent years sending scripts to agents, producers, and directors. I poured my heart and soul into it. The result was that I sold exactly zero screenplays. No one in Hollywood showed more than a passing interest in any of my stories. As the years ticked by, my patience dwindled, and my resentment grew. Along with the resentment, I started to drink more and more to fight off the anger and depression. I eventually ended up in a series of corporate jobs to pay the bills, jobs that left me feeling cold and uninspired.

By now, you know how the rest of the story unfolded; more drinking; more drugs; rock bottom.

Now clean and sober for almost five years, I decided it was time for a change -- a big change. I needed to get out of (i.e., escape) Los Angeles and live in an environment that offered serenity and beauty. I needed a new adventure and was eager to shake things up a little.

I can't remember the exact moment that I made the final decision, but at some point, I just thought: *that's it*! *I'm done*! I'd had enough of LA with its crime, potholes, and traffic. *I'm outta here!*

I was still working as a freelance marketing consultant, making decent money. I even managed to pay off all of my debt and save $18,000 (an unimaginable amount of money just a few years ago), which was enough to help me move without too much financial worry.

I sold or gave away almost everything I owned. It felt liberating to purge myself of all the material crap I had accumulated over the years. I felt lighter, like I could go anywhere, and do anything I wanted. I was unrestricted and free.

Then I spent several weeks saying goodbye to all my friends, especially all the ones I had made in AA. That was the most difficult part about leaving. I had developed some very close and meaningful relationships in the sober community. Leaving all that behind was extremely sad and a little frightening, too. Yet I knew it was time to transition into a new phase of life, which meant leaving LA once and for all.

POLLUTED

On a warm morning in July of 2011, I drove out of Los Angeles, heading for the mountains. I've been living in the Sierras ever since where I can breathe clean air, fly fish, and hike the mountains surrounding our home. When I say "our home," I'm talking about the one I share with my wife. Which leads me to the most important purpose of all...

Love

I had spent my life in and out of one bad relationship after another. All of them had been polluted by alcoholism, addiction, anger, and infidelity (sometimes I was the *cheater*, sometimes I was the *cheatee*). My romantic life was a pathetic mess, nothing more than a long list of broken promises and broken hearts, both mine and theirs. My dating life had been, to put it mildly, a complete horror show.

When I started my journey in sobriety, the very last thing I wanted to do was date, anyone. I was utterly burned-out on dating and everything that went along with it. I was also highly distrustful of other people and preferred to be alone rather than take another chance at disaster. With Paul's encouragement, I decided to take a year off from dating, which allowed me to concentrate entirely on my recovery. I didn't realize until then how much time I spent focusing on the opposite sex. Once I was able to let that part of my life go, I felt an enormous weight lift off my shoulders.

After I passed my first year of sobriety, I was so happy with the way my life was going that I decided I still wasn't ready to dip my toe back into the dating pool. So I continued forward, focusing on my recovery while working with others to help them stay sober.

However, there finally came the point when I was ready to "get back out there." What I soon discovered was that dating without the courage that alcohol provided is pretty damn weird. You have to come up with things to do and say while trying not to have a nervous breakdown. It all proved to be a lot more complicated and challenging than I remembered because I mostly didn't remember much from my days of drunk dating.

The biggest challenge I faced in this department was deciding whether or not I should date women who drank. On the one hand, most normal people drink moderately and don't have a problem with alcohol like me. However, it might make me nervous being around someone while they're drinking. I was worried that kissing someone with the scent of wine or vodka on their breath could trigger a relapse. Also, at this stage of my sobriety, I found it incredibly annoying to be around drunk people (I still do today, actually).

On the other hand, dating another recovering alcoholic would probably include all the baggage that we usually bring to the party. It is one thing to deal with my insanity and emotional instability, but dating someone with the same psychological issues could prove combustible.

I tried going both routes with mixed results. There were no fireworks, nor cupid arrows flying, but it was an interesting time, and I mostly enjoyed the experience of sober dating. Best of all, there were no broken windows, holes punched in any walls, or late-night screaming matches and complaining neighbors. My dating adventures were sometimes and sometimes dull, but without conflict or drama. Imagine that!

But "The One" never seemed to materialize.

I believe in the expression: *"Let God do for us what we can't do for ourselves."* I have found that this adage is particularly true when it comes to matters of the heart. Love seems to have its way of finding us when we least expect it and is often waiting in the most obvious places when we're unaware of its proximity.

I first noticed Dany at an AA meeting when I was in the early months of my sobriety. I was still in the middle of my dating embargo, so I never bothered to talk with her whenever we crossed paths. But I couldn't take my eyes off her. I would glance over at her constantly whenever we were in the same meeting together, especially when she smiled or laughed. I thought she was beautiful and wondered if I would ever find the courage to talk to her.

I did finally talk to Dany -- but it took three years. We were standing next to each other after a meeting when I complimented her about her new haircut. We spoke maybe ten words to each other that day, but afterwards a friendship slowly bloomed.

It only took me *another year* to ask her out on a date (I never claimed to be a fast operator).

Even after I left Los Angeles for the Sierras, we continued to date. We traveled back and forth to see each other as often as possible. Long-distance relationships have a bad reputation, but for us, it worked. In 2012, on a warm and beautiful summer day, we were married on the side of a mountain overlooking the shimmering blue expanse of Lake Tahoe.

Our wedding was joined by friends and family who had come from far and wide to celebrate the most important day of our lives. Many of the people in attendance were our dear friends from AA, who traveled from Los Angeles to celebrate our union.

Today, we live in the Sierra Mountains with our two dogs, Moonpie and Biscuit. Our marriage, like our friendship, is based on trust, mutual respect, and love. Every day and every year seems to get better. I finally found The One I had been looking for my entire life. I only had to get sober to find her.

Through sobriety, I found love. How cool is that!

WHAT IT'S LIKE NOW

Life Unpolluted

Each year since we were married, Dany and I have returned to Maui, where we had our honeymoon. Hawaii is a magical place of epic beauty. It's our "happy place." Every time I walk off the plane and breathe in the warm tropical air, a sense of joy fills my soul.

A couple of years ago, we took a charter boat along with Dany's sister, Kathy, her husband, Matt, and their daughter, Sophie, to a cove that is popular for snorkeling.

We slipped into the water and swam away from the boat. Dany and I held hands as we gazed down at the garden of coral and the numerous fish of all shapes and sizes below the surface. The rainbow of colors that swirled around us was startling. We drifted along quietly, gently rising and dropping with the ocean tide, pointing out various things to each other, amazed at everything we were seeing.

I remember thinking to myself *this is it*; *I found it. This is what I've been looking for my entire life*. I was with the person I loved, holding hands as we floated peacefully through a world of beauty, color, and life. At that moment, I was overwhelmed with gratitude. I had everything I wanted.

Sobriety has given me everything I have today. Love, health, faith, security, optimism, and joy are all a result of the journey I have taken to get clean and to experience life unpolluted by addiction.

I've been sober for more than twelve years, and my life seems to get better every year I remain in recovery. Is my life perfect or free from pain? Hell, no! There have been many challenges along the way and painful experiences to face. Life, sober or not, is difficult at times and filled with both joy and suffering. This is just how the game works. But instead of fighting against the tide, I've learned to float with it, letting it take me wherever it wants to go.

If you're struggling with addiction of any kind, I encourage you to seek the help you deserve. There is a solution to the problem you're facing. Sobriety is a gift that is being shared by thousands of people every day around the world. The only thing you need to do is ask, and the help you need will be there.

The road to recovery is often bumpy, painful, and messy, but it's well worth the journey. I hope you find your path to freedom, a life that is clean and unpolluted.

###

CAN I GET YOUR HELP?

As an independent author, I rely on reader feedback to generate awareness of my books. If you have time, I would truly appreciate your honest opinion of this book on Amazon or wherever you bought it, or social media, so other people can benefit from your opinion.

Thank you and many blessings.

Dirk Foster

Connect With Me:

Join My Newsletter and Receive a FREE BOOK at **www.thesoberjourney.com**

Facebook:
www.facebook.com/sobertravels/

Author Page:
https://www.facebook.com/Dirk-Foster-Author105017227522728/?modal=admin_todo_tour

Other Books by Dirk Foster:

The Sober Journey: A Guide to Prayer and Meditation in Recovery

Sober Body: A Guide to Health and Fitness in Sobriety

Sober and Broke: How to Make Money, Save Money, Pay Debt and Find Financial Peace is Sobriety

Printed in Great Britain
by Amazon